W9-BQZ-224

FACTS AT YOUR FINGERTIPS

GREAT SCIENTISTS
PHILOSOPHY, INVENTION, AND ENGINEERING

BROWN
BEAR
BOOKS

Published by Brown Bear Books Limited

An imprint of:
The Brown Reference Group Ltd
68 Topstone Road
Redding
Connecticut 06896
USA

www.brownreference.com

© 2009 The Brown Reference Group Ltd

Library of Congress Cataloging-in-Publication Data available upon request

ISBN-13 978-1-933834-48-1

Editorial Director: Lindsey Lowe
Managing Editor: Tim Harris
Project Director: Graham Bateman
Designer: Steve McCurdy
Editor: Derek Hall

Printed in the United States of America

Picture Credits

Abbreviations: AKG Archiv für Kunst und Geschichte, London; BAL Bridgeman Art Library; C Corbis; MEPL Mary Evans Picture Library; SPL Science Photo Library; b=bottom; c=center; t=top; l=left; r=right.

Cover Images
Front: *Thomas Edison,* Corbis/Hulton Deutsch
Back: *Aristotle,* Jupiter/Photos.com

1, 3 Photos.com; 4 Kunsthistorisches Museum, Vienna, Austria/BAL; 5t Museo Archeologico Nazionale, Naples, Italy/BAL-Roger Viollet; 5b Araldo de Luca/C; 6-7 C; 7 BPCC/Aldus Archive; 10 Scottish National Portrait Gallery, Edinburgh/BAL; 11 Waterhouse and Dodd, London/BAL; 12 Science Museum/SSPL; 13, 14t Bettmann/C; 14b Science Museum/SSPL; 15t, 15b Science Museum, London/BAL; 16 Martyn Austin/C; 18l Science Museum/SSPL; 18r Hulton/Archive; 19t, 19b, 20t, 20c Science Museum/SSPL; 22 Hulton/Archive; 24, 25t AKG; 25c Bettmann/C; 26tl Leonard de Selva/C; 26tc MEPL; 26b, 27 Bettmann/C; 29t, 29b, 31t, 31c, 32c, 32b, 34c AKG; 34b ARPL; 35 Chris Hellier/C; 37l C; 37tr Bettmann/C; 37br Underwood & Underwood/C; 38 MEPL; 38-39 Hulton/Archive; 39, 40 Bettmann/C; 42 Hulton-Deutsch Collection/C; 43 Hulton/Archive; 45 Imperial War Museum; 46 Ullstein Bilderdienst; 48 By courtesy of the National Portrait Gallery, London; 49 King's College Library, Cambridge; 50c C; 50b Hulton/Archive; 51l Bletchley Park Trust/SSPL; 51r Science Museum/SSPL; 52t, 52c Bletchley Park Trust/SSPL; 53 Science Museum/SSPL; 54 New York Times; 56, 57 Bettmann/C; 58t Omikron/SPL; 58c Hulton-Deutsch Collection/C; 58b Genevieve Naylor/C; 59t, 59b Bettmann/C; 60 Bettmann/C

Artwork © The Brown Reference Group Ltd

The Brown Reference Group Ltd has made every effort to trace copyright holders of the pictures used in this book. Anyone having claims to ownership not identified above is invited to contact The Brown Reference Group Ltd.

CONTENTS

ARISTOTLE 4–9

JAMES WATT 10–17

CHARLES BABBAGE AND
ADA LOVELACE 18–23

THOMAS ALVA EDISON 24–33

ALEXANDER GRAHAM
BELL 34–41

FRITZ HABER 42–47

ALAN TURING 48–55

JONAS SALK 56–61

Glossary/Further
Resources/Index 62–64

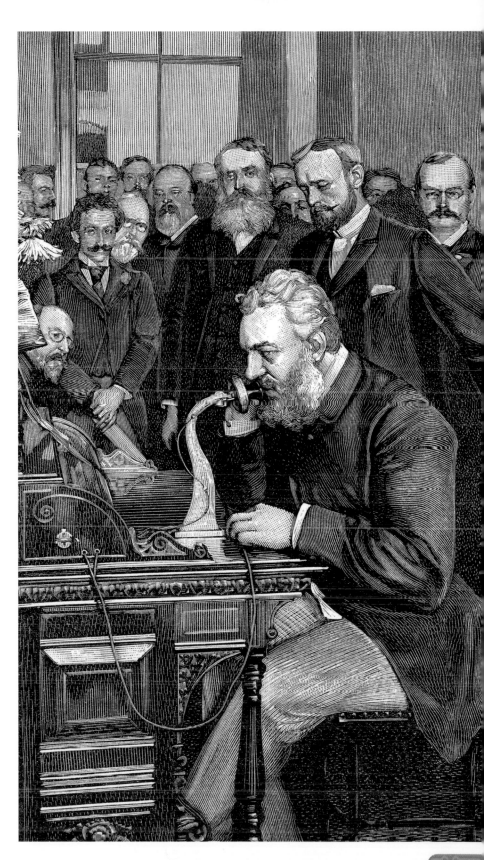

Page 1: James Watt.
This page: Alexander Graham Bell.

ARISTOTLE

384 –322 BC

"More trust should be put in the evidence of observation rather than in theories, and in theories only insofar as they are confirmed by the observed facts."

Aristotle
On the Generation of Animals
(4th century BC)

THE WRITINGS OF THE ANCIENT GREEK PHILOSOPHER ARISTOTLE SPANNED ALL BRANCHES OF HUMAN KNOWLEDGE, FROM ZOOLOGY TO POLITICS. HE ALSO MADE A LASTING IMPACT ON THE THOUGHTS AND SCIENTIFIC DISCOVERIES OF LATER CIVILIZATIONS.

Aristotle was born in 384 BC in Stagira, in Greece. In 367 BC he went to study at the Academy in Athens, founded by the philosopher Plato (c. 428–c. 348 BC). Aristotle stayed there for 20 years, after which time he went to Assos, on the coast of what is now northwest Turkey. Here he befriended another philosopher, Theophrastus (c. 372–c. 287 BC), and they moved to Mytilene, the chief city on the island of Lesbos. Aristotle studied the island's natural history. In 342 BC he returned to Macedonia to teach the Macedonian king Philip II's 14-year-old son, Alexander. After his father's death, Aristotle's royal pupil would conquer most of the known world as Alexander the Great (356–323 BC). In about 339 BC Aristotle returned to Stagira, where he continued to record as much as he could about the natural world.

Aristotle returned to Athens in 335 BC and founded his own school, the Lyceum. After Alexander's death in 323 BC there was an outbreak of anti-Macedonian feeling in Athens. Aristotle seems to have felt threatened by it, and he retired to the isle of Euboea, where he died soon afterward, in 322 BC. Theophrastus succeeded him as head of the Lyceum in Athens.

EARLY SCIENTIFIC BELIEFS

The ancient Greeks were artistic, literate, and educated, and science and philosophy had been studied from long before Aristotle's time. The founder of Greek science and philosophy was traditionally held to be Thales of Miletus (c. 624–c. 545 BC). He declared that everything was made of water, probably because he was able to observe that liquid water is transformed into air as steam and into a solid as ice. Other Greek scientists believed that all natural objects are made from four basic elements—earth, air, water, and fire—while others argued that the world is composed of indivisible units of matter they called atoms.

Greek thought was highly rational—that is, ideas

SCHOOLS OF LEARNING IN ATHENS

Permanent schools were a fairly recent development in Greece when Aristotle enrolled at Plato's Academy in 367 BC. Before then, individual teachers known as Sophists traveled throughout the Greek world, settling for short periods in a particular spot to take in a few pupils for a fee.

Like other schools in Athens, Plato's Academy was an extension of a public gymnasium: exercise was held to be a key part of the education of young Athenian males (girls were excluded, not being considered fit for schooling). It was a center for philosophical, mathematical, and scientific study.

Plato, perhaps the most influential philosopher of all time, set up his Academy in 387 BC after a long period abroad following Socrates's trial and death. Socrates (469–399 BC) had been Plato's teacher. The most famous philosopher of his day, Socrates left no writings of his own. His ideas have come down to us in the form of dialogs (conversational exchanges) written down by Plato, through which Plato also expounded his own philosophical theories. Socrates's ideas troubled many in Athens. In 399 BC he was charged with "neglect of the gods" and "corrupting the youth" of Athens, found guilty, and condemned to death by drinking hemlock, a deadly poison.

A Roman mosaic, discovered at Pompeii, shows Plato teaching at his Academy in Athens. He is using a stick to draw diagrams in the sand as he instructs fellow philosophers in the study of geometry.

Gymnasiums were places of learning where male Greek athletes over the age of 18 received training. The gymnasiums offered all-around education for young men. They could learn philosophy, music, and literature, in addition to taking part in athletics. Students often participated in public sports festivals, competing for trophies such as this ceramic bowl which has a sporting theme.

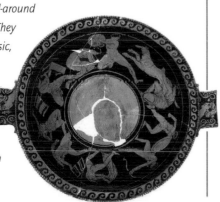

KEY DATES

384 BC Born in northern Greek colony of Stagira, the son of a physician

367 BC Moves to Athens to study at Plato's Academy

345–42 BC Devotes time to study of natural history on Lesbos

342 BC Appointed tutor to Alexander the Great in Macedonia

335 BC Returns to Athens where he establishes the Lyceum

323 BC Leaves Athens, succeeded by Theophrastus as head of Lyceum

ZOOLOGICAL STUDIES

Aristotle was the first person to try to describe the animals of the known world in a systematic way: he set about studying hundreds of creatures in order to classify and understand them. In works such as *History of Animals* and *On the Generation of Animals* he carefully noted their physical characteristics, and he also tried to consider how animals reproduce, how they move, their physical structure (anatomy), their processes and functions (physiology), and their behavior.

Aristotle was a keen observer of nature, but also believed that there was a reason plants and animals were as they were: he thought that they had natural purposes or "ends," and these dictated the forms they develop. This belief is called teleology. "Spiny lobsters have tails because they swim about," Aristotle wrote, "and so a tail is of use to them, serving them for propulsion like an oar." This view of nature was extraordinarily influential, right up until the 19th century, when the English naturalist Charles Darwin (1809–1882) showed that the characteristics developed by animals and plants come about not through preordained purpose but through "natural selection." This allows the survival of those animals and plants that are best suited to their surroundings, and the development of new species. Natural selection is often loosely referred to as "the survival of the fittest."

In his work Aristotle described more than 500 different species. He tried not to accept reports that he could not confirm: he wrote, cautiously, that "if we are to believe Ctesias [a 5th-century BC Greek historian and physician], there is such an animal as the mantichora, with a triple row of teeth in both upper and lower jaw, as big as a lion, hairy, resembling a man in its face and ears." The animal that Ctesias described so fancifully was probably an Indian tiger.

In many regards Aristotle's biological work was groundbreaking. It includes a description of the joints of an

This 18th-century etching depicts Aristotle and a colleague amidst various exotic animals. Aristotle is observing the creatures intently, making notes or sketches as he does so.

elephant's leg, discrediting the common belief that elephants had to lean against trees to sleep. He also made a detailed study of life within a beehive, which was mostly well observed, though he thought the hive was ruled by a male, not a female, bee. Aristotle's most precise and detailed work was in his study of marine life. His assertion that the female catfish left her eggs to be cared for by the male was scorned, but it was among several of his claims that 19th-century scientists found to be absolutely accurate.

were reached by systematically collecting all the known facts about a subject and placing them within an overall scheme. The high value given to literacy meant that ideas could be written down and passed around for general criticism and discussion.

LOOKING AT ARISTOTLE'S WORK

Many of Aristotle's ideas exist in the form of lecture notes or texts for students. Unlike modern scientists, Aristotle and his contemporaries did not use scientific experiments to confirm their theories. But Aristotle

Moon during an eclipse. Like most thinkers of his day, Aristotle believed that the Earth lay at the center of the universe. He believed that the stars and planets were carried on transparent spheres. According to Aristotle, the spheres rotated daily around a stationary Earth with steady circular motion but at different speeds. Beyond them an additional sphere held the fixed stars. Not all Greek thinkers agreed; for example, Aristarchus of Samos (310–230 BC) believed that the Sun, not the Earth, lay at the center of the universe. But Aristotle's system became generally accepted and was to dominate European thought until the 15th century.

Aristotle also studied motion, beginning with the theory that "Whatever is moved is moved by something." This belief influenced scientists until it was disposed of by Galileo Galilei (1564–1642) and Isaac Newton (1642–1727). Even in Aristotle's time it had its limitations, as it could be seen that many things are able to move without a mover—for instance, apples fall to the ground from trees. Aristotle thus defined three types of motion occurring on Earth. Living creatures move because they choose to ("voluntary" motion). The second kind of motion he described as "natural." He held that objects were composed of the four elements—earth, water, air, and fire. Earth, the heaviest, lay at the center of the cosmos, surrounded by water, then air, then fire. When moved from their natural place, objects try to return. This explained why air bubbles rise through water, or earth falls through air.

Aristotle noted that objects speed up as they fall, but thought this was because the nearer they got to their natural place, the greater the force attracting them. He wrongly believed that heavy objects fall faster than lighter ones, reasoning that the more matter an object contains, the more quickly it returns to its natural place. According to Aristotle's theory, an object such as an arrow would fall to the ground as soon as the "mover" (the archer) sets it in motion. As this clearly did not happen, Aristotle concluded that the medium it passed through (in this case, air) must somehow move the object. He called this "violent" motion.

Islamic scholars studied Aristotle's findings after they had been largely forgotten in the West. This is a 13th-century Arabic translation of one of Aristotle's zoological works. Translations from Arabic into Latin in the 12th century helped to reintroduce much of Aristotle's scientific work to Western scholars.

always tried to support his ideas with evidence based on his own observations and practical experience.

Aristotle was the first to prove scientifically that the Earth was shaped like a ball by observing that the shadow of the Earth is round when it appears on the

ARISTOTLE

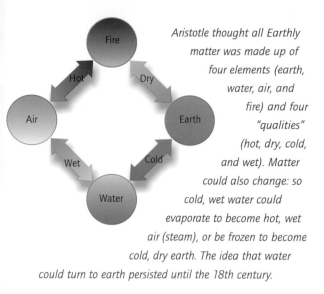

Aristotle thought all Earthly matter was made up of four elements (earth, water, air, and fire) and four "qualities" (hot, dry, cold, and wet). Matter could also change: so cold, wet water could evaporate to become hot, wet air (steam), or be frozen to become cold, dry earth. The idea that water could turn to earth persisted until the 18th century.

As already noted, Aristotle believed that heavenly bodies such as the stars and planets moved in a circular uniform motion. This form of movement was unlike any of the types of motion that take place on Earth, and from this he reasoned that the stars and planets are not subject to the laws that control the behavior of objects on Earth. Therefore, they could not be composed of the four elements of earth, water, air, and fire, but of a fifth, entirely different element. Later philosophers came to call this fifth element quintessence (from *quinta*, Latin for fifth, and *essentia*, meaning the being or essence of a thing). Aristotle divided the heavens (what we call space today) into two separate and distinct realms: the "superlunary" (above the Moon) and the "sublunary" (below the Moon). The sublunary realm was subject to the same physical and natural laws that operate on Earth, but the superlunary realm was governed by its own laws. Aristotle believed that the Earthly elements change their form by losing one of a pair of opposite properties, known as "contraries," and gaining the other (see figure, left). But quintessence does not possess these contraries. Because Aristotle believed that change requires contraries, he reasoned that there can be no change without them; therefore, he concluded, the heavens must be unchangeable. From this, he reasoned that any object moving in the skies, such as a comet or lightning, must occupy the sublunary realm.

ARISTOTELIAN LOGIC

The term "logic" (from the Greek word *logos*, meaning speech or reasoning) was first used by Xenocrates (c. 395–314 BC), but it was Aristotle who provided some of the earliest surviving and complete texts on the subject. Aspects of Aristotelian logic continue to be taught today.

One of the most famous examples of Aristotle's logic is called the "Aristotelian syllogistic." A "syllogism" is an argument based on deductive reasoning. A syllogism must have two "premises," or assumptions, from which you can draw a conclusion. For example:

All birds are two-legged
All eagles are birds
All eagles are two-legged

The first statement is the "major" premise; the second is the "minor" premise; the last line draws a conclusion. The premises can be universal ("all," or "no") or particular ("some"); must be either affirmative (all As are B), or negative (no As are B); have a sign of quantity ("all"); and must contain three terms: major (in this case, "two-legged"), minor ("eagles"), and middle ("birds").

A wrongly constructed syllogism can result in a logically flawed argument or "fallacy," as, for example:
All birds can fly; helicopters can fly; therefore helicopters are birds!

A universal, affirmative syllogism can be represented diagrammatically by three concentric circles. The major term encloses both the middle term and the minor term. Here we argue that all eagles (C) are birds (B), and thus eagles are two-legged (A).

Before 390 BC

Greek philosophers make studies of the natural world; Democritus (c. 460–c. 370 BC) develops the theory of atomism—that the world is composed of indivisible entities called atoms

c. 387 Greek philosopher Plato (c. 428–c. 348 BC) founds his Academy in Athens; studies cosmology (the origin and nature of the universe) and physiology (the processes and functions of living animals and plants)

c. 370 Eudoxus of Cnidus (408–353 BC) proposes a new model of planetary motion; he accurately calculates the length of the solar year

345–42 Aristotle studies natural history on Lesbos

336 Aristotle begins work on a comprehensive survey of all knowledge

335 Aristotle founds the Lyceum in Athens; he records his lectures in manuscript form, organizes research, and teaches

322 Theophrastus (c. 372-c. 287 BC) succeeds Aristotle as head of the Lyceum and continues Aristotle's work on natural science, producing important works on plants

After 300 BC

9th-10th centuries Writings of Aristotle and other Greek scientists translated into Arabic

12th-13th centuries Aristotle's surviving works translated into Latin

1543 Aristotle's Earth-centered view of the cosmos challenged by Nicolaus Copernicus (1473-1543) and Galileo Galilei (1564-1642)

---

390 BC **360 BC** **330 BC** **300 BC**

---

390 The Celts, or Gauls, a group of peoples from central and western Europe, invade and plunder Rome, the center of the Roman republic

c. 385 Death of Aristophanes (born c. 448 BC), one of the most prolific of Greek playwrights, said to have written 54 plays, of which only 11 survive

359 Philip II (382–336 BC) becomes King of Macedonia

356 The temple of Artemis at Ephesus (in modern-day western Turkey) is burned down; it was one of the seven wonders of the ancient world

336 Philip II is assassinated; his son Alexander (356-323 BC) succeeds to the Macedonian throne

332 Alexander takes over Egypt and founds the city of Alexandria; he becomes known as Alexander the Great

331 Alexander the Great conquers the Persian empire

323 Alexander the Great dies, aged 32

323 The great museum at Alexandria is founded by Ptolemy (d. 283 BC), a former general in Alexander's army, who becomes governor of Egypt

312 The first aqueduct in Rome is completed to bring a supply of pure drinking water into the city

305 Ptolemy begins ruling in Egypt as Ptolemy I and founds a new dynasty of pharaohs

JAMES WATT

1736–1819

"Nature can be conquered if we can but find her weak side."

James Watt

JAMES WATT IMPROVED THE DESIGN OF THE FIRST STEAM ENGINE, BUILT IN 1712 BY ENGLISH INVENTOR THOMAS NEWCOMEN (1663-1729). THE STEAM ENGINE BECAME A VITAL PART OF THE INDUSTRIAL REVOLUTION, WHICH STARTED IN BRITAIN IN THE EARLY 1800s AND SPREAD TO CONTINENTAL EUROPE AND THE UNITED STATES.

James Watt was born on January 19, 1736, in Greenock, Scotland. He was a sickly child, so his mother taught him at home. He was bright and inquisitive, and spent hours taking his toys apart and putting them back together again. Watt failed to do well when he attended the local grammar school, and it was only at the age of 13 that his ability began to emerge, when he was introduced to mathematics. At home he spent his spare time building models. He also developed an interest in ships' instruments.

At the age of 17 Watt decided to become an instrument-maker, and in 1755 he traveled to London to begin learning the trade. He returned to Scotland in 1757, where he set up a business in Glasgow making and repairing instruments, including compasses and weighing scales. One of his duties was to make mathematical instruments for Glasgow University.

In 1764 Watt was asked to repair a model of a Newcomen engine (see box page 12). He soon spotted a problem with Newcomen's basic design. Steam was being wasted because the cylinder was losing too much heat through the walls, and so the engine came quickly to a stop. Watt decided he could improve the efficiency of the Newcomen engine by introducing a second chamber in which the steam could be condensed. This would allow the working cylinder to keep its heat throughout the process.

HARNESSING THE POWER OF AIR

Watt's engine was the culmination of centuries of experimentation and design. People long ago were using air (the atmosphere) to perform various tasks, even if they were not aware of it. For example, suction pumps had been used since Roman times to raise water, but it took Italian physicist Evangelista Torricelli (1608-1647) to explain how they worked.

James Watt's fascination with steam seems to have begun at an early age, as we learn from this story, recorded by his cousin, Mrs. Campbell.

"Sitting one evening with his aunt, Mrs. Muirhead, at the tea table, she said: 'James Watt, I never saw such an idle boy; take a book or employ yourself usefully; for the last hour you have not spoken a word, but taken off the lid of that kettle and put it on again, holding now a cup

This painting depicts the tale told by James Watt's cousin. The young James is lost in concentration as he watches steam condensing on a spoon.

and now a silver spoon over the steam, watching how it rises from the spout, and catching and connecting the drops of hot water it falls into. Are you not ashamed of spending your time this way?'"

Suction pumps are made up of a cylinder enclosing a piston. When the piston is raised, a partial vacuum is created, and atmospheric pressure pushes water into the cylinder. The water then escapes through an outlet and the process is repeated. It was known that pumps could lift water no more than 32 feet (9.75 m): to raise water higher than this, two or more pumps are needed on successive levels. Torricelli showed this was because the weight of the atmosphere and the weight of the

KEY DATES

1755	Began apprenticeship as an instrument maker in London
1769	Granted patent on separate condenser
1781	Patent granted on sun-and-planet gear wheel
1782	Designs double-acting rotary engine
1785	Made a fellow of the Royal Society, London

THE ATMOSPHERIC ENGINE

A drawing of the Newcomen atmospheric engine (left), built at a waterworks on the River Thames, London, in about 1730. The size of the machine can be judged by looking at the man standing near the pump handle on the left.

7 Action pulls down rocking beam on piston side and works pump on other side

6 Piston drops down as partial vacuum is created

3 Steam pushes piston up

4 Cold water is injected to condense the steam

2 Boiler produces steam

1 Water is heated

5 Water runs out

The first patented steam engine was built in 1698 by English engineer Thomas Savery (c. 1650–1715) to pump water out of mines. In 1712 a better engine was designed by Thomas Newcomen, an ironmonger working in the mines of Cornwall in southwest England.

In Newcomen's engine (right), water is heated in a boiler to produce steam. This passes into a cylinder containing a piston. The hot steam expands within the cylinder, pushing the piston up. Cold water is then injected into the cylinder, cooling the steam, which condenses into water. Because a cubic foot of steam condenses into only one cubic inch of water, a partial vacuum (a space empty of air) is created in the cylinder. As air pushes into the top of the cylinder to fill the vacuum, the atmospheric pressure forces the piston down. The piston is connected to a rocking beam. From the other side of the beam a pump handle runs down into the

mineshaft. As the piston falls, pulling one side of the beam down toward it, the beam on the other side rises, working the pump and drawing water from the shaft.

The engine was a marvel of its time, but it needed to heat water and then cool the steam every stroke, so it consumed a lot of fuel. In 1765 Watt's simple adaptation of the Newcomen engine—adding a separate condenser so that the cylinder remained hot and the condenser stayed cool throughout the operation—cut fuel costs by 75 percent.

water in the cylinder are in balance at this height, so the water cannot be lifted any higher.

Torricelli predicted that if the atmosphere had to balance a heavier liquid, the liquid would reach a much lower height. This was confirmed in 1643 by Vincenzo Viviani (1622–1703), who showed that mercury (which is 14 times heavier than water) would stand 14 times lower. It was clear that the atmosphere had power.

In 1650 German engineer and physicist Otto von Guericke (1602–1686) joined together two large copper hemispheres, and pumped out the air inside them to create a vacuum. Von Guericke then arranged for two teams of eight horses to try and pull the hemispheres apart. They failed. This was because there was no pressure inside the hemispheres; the only force acting on them was the external weight, or pressure, of the atmosphere. When air reentered the hemispheres, they fell apart by themselves.

WATT DEVELOPS HIS STEAM ENGINE

To develop his engine commercially, Watt needed financing and access to a big engineering works. In 1768 he entered into partnership with John Roebuck (1718–1794), the owner of an ironworks. The following year Watt took out a patent for his new steam engine. A patent is a licence that allows an inventor—for a limited time—to be the only person to make, use, and sell his or her invention. Watt's patent was for "A New Invented Method of Lessening the Consumption of Steam and Fuel in Fire Engines."

In 1773 Roebuck went bankrupt, and sold his interest in Watt's engine to English engineer Matthew Boulton (1728–1809), the owner of a manufacturing business in Birmingham. Boulton could see the great opportunities for trade in the Industrial Revolution that was just beginning in England. Watt's partnership with Boulton lasted 25 years and gave him the financial backing to make rapid progress with his engine.

Watt's patent was extended by the British government, and from 1776 many of his engines were installed to pump water from mines, particularly in the copper and tin mines of Cornwall. Boulton began to encourage Watt to replace the action of the original machine, which used an up-and-down motion known to

Otto von Guericke shows the power of atmospheric pressure: two teams of eight horses are unable to pull the hemispheres apart. Guericke also showed that sound does not travel in a vacuum, and that a vacuum cannot support combustion (burning) or animal life.

engineers as "reciprocating." With this type of motion energy is used first to accelerate the piston and then to stop it. As any bicyclist knows, this wastes energy: much less effort is needed to keep a bicycle moving forward at a steady speed—by turning your legs in a circle (rotary motion)—than to get it moving after a stop by pumping your legs up and down. The simplest way to produce rotary motion is by using a crank, such as those used, for example, in modern car engines. The crank converts the reciprocating motion of the cylinders into circular motion at the drive shaft, and then the wheels. Unfortunately for Watt, a patent on the crank had already been awarded in 1780 to another inventor. So instead of using a crank, Watt created other linking devices, including the sun-and-planet gear wheel, which transformed up-and-down motion into rotary motion.

In Watt's original design for his steam engine, steam operated on one side of the piston only. In 1782 he patented a method to allow steam to be admitted and condensed on both sides of the piston, so doubling the engine's output by producing power on both the up and the down strokes of the piston. The engine needed a new method of securing the piston to the beam. Watt

solved the problem with an arrangement of rods that he described as "one of the most ingenious, simple pieces of mechanism I have contrived."

In 1794 Watt and Boulton set up the firm of Boulton & Watt and built a factory for making steam engines more efficiently. Watt's patents were due to run out in 1800, after which other people could build steam engines, so he wanted to prepare for the competition. By 1800 Boulton and Watt's company had built about 500 engines, most of which were of the rotary motion type. They soon became used by a range of industries.

HIGH-PRESSURE ENGINES

Watt's engines, which worked at low temperatures and low steam pressures, were large and cumbersome. Higher steam pressure, produced at greater temperatures, would raise the energy efficiency of the engine, but Watt thought that such engines were dangerous and brought the risk of explosions. He refused to work on the development of high-pressure engines, and because the terms of his steam engine patent were so broad, no one else could develop them either. Watt's opposition to high-pressure engines prevented other inventors from developing an improved steam engine for about 20 years.

Boulton and Watt made constant improvements to their engines. This design of 1802 uses a bell crank, a two-armed lever that converts reciprocating motion into rotary motion.

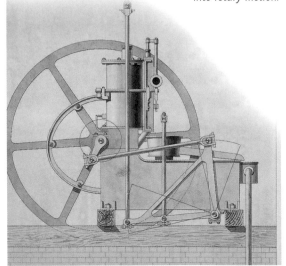

Watt's double-acting rotative beam engine; this version dates from about 1800. The engine incorporates Watt's separate condenser and air pump and his "sun-and-planet" gear wheel (which can be seen at bottom right in the picture). In this system a strut carrying the planet gear wheel is pushed up and down by the beam attached to the engine piston. The small planet gear wheel then revolves around the sun gear wheel, pushing that around and so transforming up-and-down motion into rotary motion.

Richard Trevithick (1771–1833) was an enthusiast for high-pressure engines. In 1801, after Watt's patent ran out, he built his first steam carriage, which he drove up a hill in Cornwall, and in 1802 took out a patent for high-pressure engines for stationary and locomotive use. Trevithick had developed an ingenious safety measure against explosions. A safety valve on the boiler did not always guarantee protection; workers often screwed the valves down to make the machines easier to operate, increasing the risk of explosion. Trevithick's answer was to use lead rivets; these melted when the water reached a certain temperature, allowing steam to escape.

Watt's engines, with huge cylinders 7 feet (2 m) in diameter, were far too unwieldy to be used for

Richard Trevithick's railroad in Euston Square, London, from a contemporary sketch. It shows his third engine, named the Catch me who can, *which he demonstrated to an eager public in 1808. With its coachload of passengers, the train reached a speed of 10 miles per hour (16 km/h).*

transportation; the advantage of Trevithick's high-pressure engine was that it was smaller, lighter, and more efficient in fuel and energy. By 1804, Trevithick had built the first steam-powered locomotive and used it to haul a load of iron and 70 men a distance of 10 miles (16 km). Trevithick was a talented engineer who made many improvements to boiler design and construction. But although his high-pressure engine was to prove highly versatile, it brought him no financial profit.

Richard Trevithick
1771–1833

Trevithick taught himself engineering. Between 1801 and 1815 he built steam road carriages, stationary steam engines, and the world's first steam railway locomotive. He also invented the Cornish pumping engine, which soon replaced Watt's machines. In 1816 Trevithick traveled to South America to sell his engines. While there he fished for pearls, prospected for minerals, and fought in the wars of liberation alongside the revolutionary leader Simón Bolívar (1783–1830). Eventually, Trevithick returned to England, but died penniless.

Oliver Evans
1755–1819

Oliver Evans was born in Newport, Delaware. His interest in steam power derived from a book describing the Newcomen engine. Evans began to think about using high-pressure steam to drive vehicles as early as 1777, and in 1812 he predicted that one day a person would be able to leave Washington in the morning and arrive in New York on the same day. In 1785 Evans installed the first continuous production line in a flour mill. Evans's mill was driven by water power, which was also used to grind the corn and carry the grain through the mill by way of a system of elevators, hoppers, and belts, "without the aid of human labor." Evans later built steamboats. Like Watt and others, much of Evans's later life was spent in court defending patents and pursuing the pirates who infringed his rights.

Steam engines were a key factor in the development of ship transportation, especially in the United States, where river steamboats drastically cut shipping times and costs. This 19th-century engraving depicts a paddle steamer cruising along the Mississippi River, near Baton Rouge in Louisiana.

CALCULATING PAYMENTS

Trevithick's lack of business sense was in marked contrast to Watt, who made a considerable amount of money from his invention. However, Watt was forced to spend time and money in court to defend his patents.

Watt's engines were first used in collieries and ironworks. Boulton & Watt designed and supervised the building of the engine, while the customer paid the material and building costs. Profits were calculated on how much fuel their clients saved by using one of their machines. A different method of payment was devised for the rotary engine, which operated mills of various kinds. Watt worked out that a horse, the previous source of mill power, could raise 33,000 pounds by one foot in one minute (14,969 kg by 0.3 m in one minute), a measure Watt called horsepower or hp. Millowners paid a charge based on how many horsepower per year were provided by Watt's rotary engines.

STILL WORKING IN RETIREMENT

Watt was married twice: first to his cousin Margaret Miller, with whom he had six children. After her death he married Ann MacGregor, with whom he had two more children. He had a wide interest in instrument-making and scientific invention, and when he retired in 1800, he fitted out the garret of his home near Birmingham as a workshop. He died there on August 25, 1819, aged 83.

Before 1740

English engineer Thomas Savery (c. 1650–1715) patents first steam engine; Thomas Newcomen (1663-1729) uses atmospheric pressure to drive his 1712 steam engine

1744 American scientist Benjamin Franklin (1706–1790) invents the Franklin stove, which uses hot air to heat a room

1747 The first civil engineering school, the School for Bridges and Highways, is established in France

1752 English engineer James Brindley (1716-1772) devises a water engine for draining a coal mine

1764 James Hargreaves (c. 1720-1778) invents the spinning jenny, which can spin many threads at the same time

1765 James Watt builds the first model of his steam engine with separate condenser

1769 English industrialist Richard Arkwright (1732–1792) invents a spinning frame that produces a strong warp thread

1774 English inventor and manufacturer John Wilkinson (1728-1808) develops a machine that can bore cylinders for Boulton & Watt's steam engines

1782 Watt patents his double-acting steam engine

1785 English inventor Edmund Cartwright (1743-1823) builds the first power loom

1800 English engineer Richard Trevithick (1771-1833) builds his first high-pressure steam engine

1807 The first practical steamboat, the *Clermont*, is built by American engineer Robert Fulton (1765-1815); it makes its maiden voyage from Manhattan to Clermont, NY

1814 English engineer George Stephenson (1781-1848) develops his first steam engine

---

(1740)   (1760)   (1780)   (1800)

1755 The first ever *Dictionary of the English Language*, by the English lexicographer and writer Dr Samuel Johnson (1709–84), is published.

1763 The area of Canada still under French rule is passed over to the English under the Treaty of Paris

1765 The Stamp Act, passed by the British Parliament, taxes items such as newspapers, dice, and playing cards, and is the first direct tax to be imposed on the American colonists

1775 In Britain, bond labor by women and children is ended in salt and coal mines

1781 The American Revolution ends on October 19, though the British continue to hold New York until 1783

1787 George Washington (1732-1799) chairs the constitutional convention in Philadelphia that formulates a constitution for the newly created United States of America

1789 George Washington becomes the first chief-magistrate or president of the new United States government

1811 The first major novel by English writer Jane Austen (1775-1817), *Sense and Sensibility*, is published anonymously in London

1813 In Britain, leaders of the Luddite movement—textile workers who smash the new looms they fear will put them out of work—are hanged or transported to Australia

1821 Napoleon dies on the island of Saint Helena in the South Atlantic, having been exiled there in 1815

CHARLES BABBAGE AND ADA LOVELACE

1792–1871 & 1815–1852

"The whole of the developments and operations of analysis are now capable of being executed by machinery... As soon as an Analytical Engine exists, it will necessarily guide the future course of science."

Charles Babbage
Passages from the Life of a Philosopher
(1864)

CHARLES BABBAGE, AN ENGLISH MATHEMATICIAN, BELIEVED IT WOULD BE POSSIBLE TO CREATE AN "ANALYTICAL ENGINE" THAT COULD STORE INFORMATION AND WORK FROM A SET OF INSTRUCTIONS. MUCH LATER, BABBAGE'S IDEAS INFLUENCED THE MODERN COMPUTER REVOLUTION. ADA LOVELACE CREATED THE FIRST COMPUTER PROGRAM FOR HIS ENGINE.

Charles Babbage was born on December 26, 1791, probably in London, England. He attended several schools before returning home to be tutored in the subject he liked best: mathematics. In 1810 he entered Cambridge University, graduating in 1814. He married in that year, and moved to London.

In 1812, while at Cambridge, Babbage and the English astronomer John Herschel (1792–1871) helped form the Analytical Society, which aimed to introduce modern mathematical methods into the university. The problem lay with the calculus, the branch of mathematics discovered by English scientist Sir Isaac Newton (1642–1727) and German philosopher and mathematician Gottfried Leibniz (1646–1716). Whereas the signs and symbols used by mathematicians in continental Europe were based on those developed by Leibniz, most British scientists followed Newton's method. However, Newton's was more cumbersome than Leibniz's, and the development of the calculus in Britain lagged behind continental Europe. Babbage, who had learned Leibniz's system, wanted others to do the same.

SIMPLIFYING CALCULATIONS

Since ancient times, people have tried various methods to simplify calculations. One of the earliest devices, the abacus, is still in use in many parts of the world. It usually consists of rows of movable beads strung on rods or wires within a frame, the position of the beads indicating numerical values.

In addition to the calculus, another important aid to calculation, known as "logarithms," was invented in 1614 by John Napier (1550–1617), a Scottish mathematician. They provided a means of carrying out complicated sums, and were particularly helpful to those having to carry out difficult calculations quickly, such as navigators and astronomers. Logarithms of numbers were worked out and written down in logarithm tables. To multiply two numbers, their logarithms were just added together. The logarithm of the total could then be looked up in the table. Although logarithms saved a great deal of time in making calculations, it was clear that if calculation could be mechanized, the process could be speeded up even further. In 1642–1644 French philosopher Blaise Pascal (1623–1662) invented the first digital calculating machine; the design was later refined by Leibniz.

In 1819 Babbage began to think about how to use mechanical methods to undertake more advanced mathematical calculations. He was inspired by a passage in the *Wealth of Nations* (1776) by the Scottish economist Adam Smith (1723–1790). Smith pointed out that if one man working alone had to manufacture pins, he would find it difficult to finish one pin a day. But if each employee carried out just one part of the process, it would speed it up greatly. Smith reported that he had seen a factory of 10 men produce 48,000 pins a day.

KEY DATES

1812 Charles Babbage jointly founds Analytical Society

1816 Elected to the Royal Society

1823 Babbage begins work on Difference Engine

1832 Publishes *On the Economy of Machinery and Manufactures*

1834 Begins work on Analytical Engine

1864 Publishes *Passages from the Life of a Philosopher*

1834 Ada Lovelace attends public lecture given by Charles Babbage

1835 Marries William King, later Earl of Lovelace

1843 Lovelace publishes *Sketch of the Analytical Engine Invented by Charles Babbage*

1980 U.S. Department of Defense names programming language ADA for her

Part of Babbage's original Difference Engine (top). The Difference Engine above was built using Babbage's 1847–49 drawings, and was completed in 1991. It can be seen in the Science Museum in London.

John Napier
1550–1617

John Napier was born in Scotland. He entered St. Andrews University, but seems to have left quite quickly, and began traveling abroad. By 1571 he had returned to Scotland. A fervent Protestant, Napier urged King James VI of Scotland (1566-1625) to stand up to Roman Catholicism. He began designing war machines when it was feared that Spain would invade Scotland. Napier devoted his spare time to mathematics. He is best known for the tables of logarithms he compiled. He also invented a calculating tool that used small rods, known as Napier's bones, that were moved by hand. In the version shown right, rotating cylinders have replaced the rods.

Babbage wondered if Smith's approach could be applied to mathematical calculation. He saw a link with the work of the French mathematician François de Prony (1755-1839). The metric system had been introduced in France in the 1790s. To prepare the new mathematical tables needed to serve the metric system, de Prony organized his workers on an assembly line, with each worker performing simple additions or subtractions. Because the labor was divided into easy, repeated operations, Babbage decided that the workers were acting "mechanically." So why not replace workers with a mechanical calculating machine?

THE DIFFERENCE ENGINE

Babbage set out to build a machine based on what was known as the "method of differences." This can be explained by seeing how it can be used to construct a table of cubes. Cubes are numbers that have been multiplied by themselves three times: for example, 4 x 4 x 4 = 64 (usually written as 4^3). In the table right, a list of consecutive numbers from 1–6 is shown on the left. The cube of each number is shown beside it, the difference between each cube and the next lower cube is in the next column, and so on, until a constant difference of 6 has been reached. The arrows show the path by which each difference is calculated.

You can use the table to work out further cubes "mechanically," using addition. The arrows show the paths that the additions should take. To find the cube of the next number, 7, the constant 6 has to be added to the second difference of the previous number, 6. So, as you can see in the table, 6 is added to 30 to get 36. Following the arrows again: 36 + 91 = 127; 127 + 216 = 343. That is the cube of 7; the same procedure gives us the cube of 8 (which is 512), and so on.

From this Babbage knew that a skillful engineer could design a system of cogwheels and rods that could be used to work out further cubes. Babbage began work on his Difference Engine, as he named it, in 1823. A demonstration model was built. Once the machine was started, it did not need further human intervention: in this sense, it can be described as the first automatic calculator. It was, however, very limited in scope. Inspired by Babbage's work, two Swedish engineers, Georg Scheutz (1795-1873) and Edvard, his son (1821-1881), built a number of simplified Difference Engines. One was purchased by the Dudley Observatory in Albany, New York, and is now in the Smithsonian Institution in Washington, D.C.

Number	Cube	First	Second	Third
1	1			
2	8	7		
3	27	19	12	6
4	64	37	18	6
5	125	61	24	6
6	216	91	30	6

ADDING WITH COGWHEELS

Simple additions to create values below 10 can be made using a gear wheel with 10 cogs numbered from 0 to 9 (Fig. 1). An initial mark represents the starting point (SP). It is aligned with 0. By moving the wheel three cogs clockwise, the cog numbered 3 is aligned with the SP. If the wheel is rotated a further 5 cogs, the SP will align with the number 8. So 5 and 3 added together make 8. However, if we wish to add a further 5, the number aligned with the SP will be 3, whereas we know that 8 and 5 equals 13.

So the problem was how to create a machine that carried units over into tens. Many mechanical solutions were tried. The simplest system had gear ratios of 10 cogs to

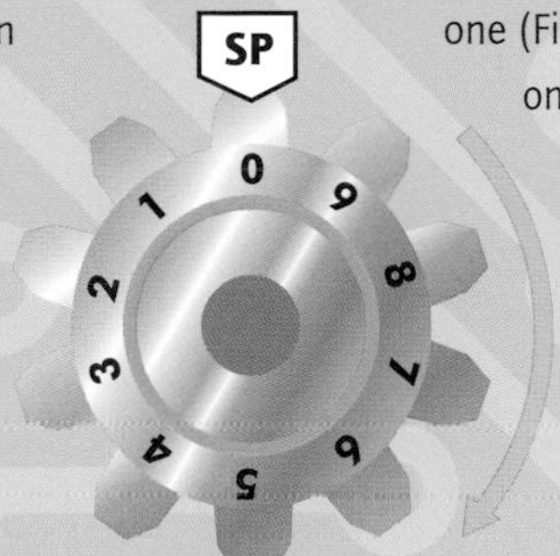

Fig. 1. Gear wheel with 10 cogs

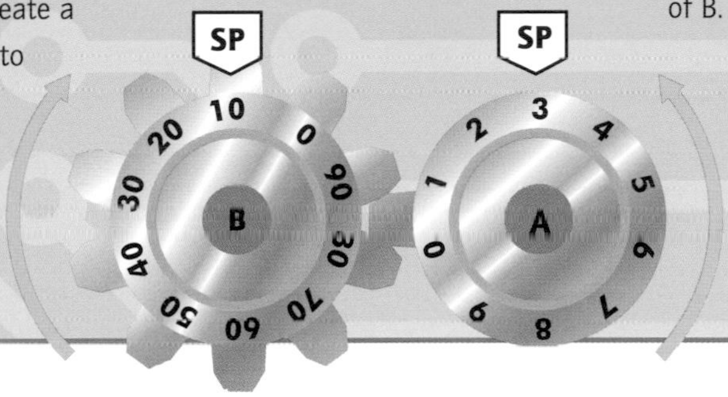

Fig. 2. Gear wheels with ratio of 10 cogs to one

one (Fig. 2). Here B has 10 cogs, while A has just one. When A makes a full revolution, B turns just one-tenth of a revolution, so 10 revolutions of wheel A will force just one complete turn of wheel B. To add 8 and 5, B is set at 0 and A at 8, and A is rotated five places. This moves the number 10 to the SP on B, and the number 3 to the SP on A, making a total of 13.

To make additions creating values running into the hundreds, further similarly geared wheels can be added to the shaft of B. Theoretically, the process can be carried on for ever, though adding extra shafts and gears inevitably increases the risk of mechanical failure.

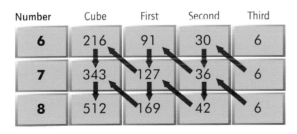

Number	Cube	First	Second	Third
6	216	91	30	6
7	343	127	36	6
8	512	169	42	6

In 1834 work on the Difference Engine was halted as spiraling costs hit the project. Babbage had put a great deal of his own money into the project, but so had the government in the form of grants, which now decided that enough was enough. By now Babbage had begun to plan a more ambitious design, for a general-purpose programmable computer that he called his Analytical Engine. In theory the machine would be able to add, subtract, multiply, and divide any number of times in any order. It would also contain a memory store and a processing unit. The operating system (what we would now refer to as software) would be

provided by punched cards, a device that had been developed initially for use in the weaving industry. However, when Babbage approached the government for a financial grant to make this machine, it seems he was told that funds were not forthcoming.

THE FIRST COMPUTER PROGRAMMER

In the same year that work on the old engine was halted, Babbage met Ada Lovelace (1815–1852), who had come to hear him lecture. She was a most unusual figure in 19th-century Britain: a well-connected young woman who had also received a sound scientific education. Ada Lovelace was the daughter of the poet Lord Byron (1788–1824), a figure adored for his verses but censored for his scandalous private life. In 1815 Byron had married a wealthy heiress, Annabella Milbanke (1792–1860). Because of her interest in mathematics, he called Annabella "the princess of parallelograms." The marriage lasted only a year, but before they separated Annabella gave birth to Ada.

Soon afterward Byron left England for good, and Ada never saw her father again.

Annabella feared that Ada would inherit the weaknesses she saw in her former husband's character. A doctor told her that the child should be taught science and mathematics to keep her "passions" under control. Encouraged by her domineering mother, Ada taught herself geometry and was trained in astronomy and mathematics. Her tutors included Augustus de Morgan (1806–1871), first professor of mathematics at London University.

Babbage became Lovelace's correspondent and friend. Their meeting had important consequences for them both. In 1842, the Italian engineer Luigi Menabrea (1809–1896) published an account of Babbage's Analytical Engine. Babbage suggested that Lovelace should translate it into English, and add her own observations. In Lovelace's version she showed how the Analytical Engine could be programmed, using punched cards, to generate an endless sequence of a class of numbers known to mathematicians as Bernoulli numbers. "The Analytical Engine," she wrote, "weaves algebraic patterns, just as the Jacquard loom weaves flowers and leaves." For her development of this idea, Lovelace is often described as the first computer programmer.

IMPROVEMENT AND CHANGE

By 1851 Babbage had "given up all expectation" of being able to construct the Analytical Engine; it had only ever existed as notes and drawings. He kept revising his initial design of 1837, however, and his last plans for the Analytical Engine were produced as late as 1871. He left over 6,000 pages of notes and some 300 engineering drawings of the machine.

The mathematician John Moulton has left an account of a visit he made with Babbage. First he was shown parts of the original Difference Engine and told, "I have not finished it because while working at it I came on the idea of my Analytical Engine, which would do all that it was capable of doing and much more so I turned my attention to the Analytical Engine." Moulton

A portrait of Ada Lovelace, from about 1840. The computer language ADA was named in her honor.

was then taken into a room full of parts for the Analytical Engine. Again Babbage told Moulton that he had not finished it because a much better idea had come to him. In a third room Moulton saw parts for another unfinished machine!

Babbage was a modernizer. New industries were emerging; if they were to be developed properly, Babbage believed that new institutions, new technologies, and new attitudes to science were needed. He insisted that the institutions of British science were desperately in need of reform. He repeated his concern that British mathematics was hopelessly backward, and that the more powerful and simpler methods used in continental Europe were allowing French mathematics to flourish in contrast.

Babbage also considered the role of science in society in his work, *On the Economy of Machinery and Manufactures* (1832). Unlike earlier economists, Babbage concentrated more on industry than agriculture. He put forward proposals he thought would help modernize Britain: decimal currency, performance-related pay, and time-and-motion studies. He was far ahead of his time—it would be another 150 years before these ideas would be introduced.

A BELATED RECOGNITION

It is said that Babbage and Lovelace began to bet heavily on horses with an "infallible" system they had developed, but this is unsupported by any evidence. However, Lovelace was deeply in debt by 1851. She was also addicted to laudanum, a liquid form of opium used as a painkiller. She died of cancer in 1852, aged 36.

Babbage died in London in 1871. Although he continued to work until his death on his Analytical Engine, it remained unbuilt (although it has since been constructed from his original plans). Babbage's contributions to computing were forgotten for many years, but he is now credited with having conceived the first automatic digital computer.

Before 1800

Scottish mathematician John Napier (1550–1617) invents logarithms

Isaac Newton (1642–1727) and Gottfried Leibniz (1646–1716), English and German mathematicians, discover calculus independently

1792 Charles Babbage is born in London

1801 German mathematician Karl Gauss (1777–1855) creates the basis of modern number theory (the study of whole numbers)

1815 Ada Lovelace is born in London

1816 Babbage is elected a fellow of the Royal Society

1823 Babbage begins work on the Difference Engine, a device for calculating logarithm values and trigonometric functions

1834 Babbage describes the first computer, his Analytical Engine

1843 Lovelace publishes a translation of Menabrea's account of the Analytical Engine, with her own additions

1847 The Institute of Mechanical Engineers is founded in England

1847 Babbage designs his Difference Engine Mark 2

1852 Lovelace dies, aged 36

1864 Babbage publishes his book, *Passages from the Life of a Philosopher*

After 1880

1946 ENIAC (the Electronic Numerical Integrator and Computer) is the first all-electronic digital computer

1948 The invention of the transistor; it will later revolutionize computers by allowing miniaturization

1958 Fortran II, the first widely used computer programming language, is introduced in the United States

---

1800 | **1820** | **1840** | **1860**

1801 The Act of Union sees the creation of the United Kingdom of Great Britain and Ireland

1804 Napoleon Bonaparte (1769–1821) is named emperor of France

1821 South American revolutionary leader Simon Bolívar (1783–1830) becomes president of Colombia; within three years he will also be ruler in Ecuador and Peru

1837 Victoria (1819–1901) becomes queen of Great Britain

1841 The American editor and politician Horace Greeley (1811–1872) founds the *New York Tribune* daily newspaper

1844 On May 24, the American inventor Samuel Finley Breese Morse (1791–1872) sends the first telegraph message from Washington to Baltimore

1853 American inventor Elisha Otis (1811–1861) patents his "elevator," with its spring-operated safety catch to prevent sudden falls

1857 A rebellion against British rule in India known as the Indian Mutiny takes place

1863 American president Abraham Lincoln (1809–1865) orders slaves in America to be set free; the decision is ratified by Congress in December 1865

1867 The U.S. government purchases Alaska from Russia

THOMAS ALVA EDISON

1847–1931

"There ain't no rules around here! We're trying to accomplish something!"

Thomas Edison

PERHAPS THE GREATEST INVENTOR OF ALL TIME, THOMAS EDISON TOOK OUT MORE THAN 1,000 PATENTS. HIS INVENTIONS HELPED CREATE THE MODERN AMERICAN WAY OF LIFE AND INCLUDE THE INCANDESCENT ELECTRIC LIGHT BULB, THE MOVIE PROJECTOR, THE ELECTRIC TYPEWRITER, AND THE EARLY GRAMOPHONE OR "PHONOGRAPH."

Thomas Edison's father ran a successful lumber business in Milan, Ohio. However, when the Lake Shore Railroad was completed in 1854 it bypassed Milan, commercially crippling the region. So the family moved to Port Huron, Michigan, where they continued to trade profitably in lumber and grain.

Edison began school when he was eight years old but learned little there. After only three months, on hearing that a teacher had described him as "addled," his mother removed him from school and taught him at home herself for the next few years. Thereafter, Edison, like English scientist Michael Faraday (1791–1867) before him, was partly self taught, learning from books and from ceaseless experimentation. Unlike Faraday, Edison had a strong business head and a drive to succeed on a wider stage.

These characteristics were immediately evident when he took his first job at age 12 as a newsboy selling papers on the new Detroit–Port Huron railroad. To supplement his earnings, he began selling fruit and candy to the passengers and soon had other boys working for him. One day he noticed an empty freight car on the train. By now, Edison had earned enough to buy a hand printing press, which he set up in the car. He wrote, printed, and sold 400 copies of his own newssheet, which he named the *Grand Trunk Herald*. There is little doubt that, if he had wanted to, Edison could have turned his abilities to creating a great retail empire. However, he was more interested in invention and in manufacturing the items he invented.

In 1863 Edison began work in the Port Huron telegraph office as an apprentice telegrapher. In comparison with modern communication methods, the electric telegraph seems a strange and very cumbersome system. Yet in its day it had an enormous impact on business and society.

MESSAGES FROM FAR AWAY

The word "telegraph" means the transmission, or sending, of a message by signal over a distance. From earliest times, simple but urgent messages, such as warnings of invasion, were conveyed by lighting beacon fires on hilltops, or by smoke or drum signals. Toward the end of the 18th century the French engineer Claude Chappe (1763-1805) invented a way of sending more detailed messages by a system of hand-operated pivoting arms. Although the arms carried lights that allowed the signals to be used at night, the system still needed relay stations at regular distances, and could be hampered by bad weather. It was little used outside France.

The first developments in electric telegraphy began in early Victorian England. The German physicist Hans Oersted (1777-1851) had shown that an electric current flowing through a wire produces a magnetic field, which can then turn a compass needle, and in 1838 English inventor William Cooke (1806-1879) and physicist Charles Wheatstone (1802-1875) used this principle to develop the five-needle telegraph (see

Workers in a telegraph office, from an 1880 engraving (above). A cartoon (left) showing a telegraph pole poking up through a living room floor suggested nowhere was immune from the new technology.

KEY DATES

1859	Edison starts work at age 12 on the newly opened Port Huron-Detroit railway as a newsboy
1863	Starts work as telegrapher
1868	Joins Western Union in Boston, Massachusetts
1869	Sets up as freelance inventor
1878	Forms Edison Electric Light Company
1892	General Electric Company founded
1914–18	Works on research projects for U.S. Navy

Chappe's optical telegraph, as depicted in a magazine illustration (far left). It used pivoting arms to send messages. The first electric telegraph was invented by Cooke and Wheatstone and was known as the five-needle system (left). To form messages, two moving needles were directed toward letters on a board. To work out the letter being sent, the receiver traced the lines running from the two pointers and noted where they intersected.

The most commonly used letters required the fewest symbols: e is indicated by a single dot, for example. The word EDISON is spelled: . (E) –.. (D) .. (I) ... (S) – – – (O) – . (N). To send the message, an operator key was depressed to complete an electric circuit. At first, the dots and dashes were embossed on a paper roll as they were received, but later a "sounding" key was developed so that a skilled operator at the other end was able to decode the message by listening to the "clicks" coming over the wire.

SPREADING THE TELEGRAPH NETWORK

The electric telegraph spread rapidly. The first line, opened in 1844, linked Washington and Baltimore. By 1866 an underwater cable connected countries on either side of the Atlantic Ocean. The new telegraph industry created a group of young men fascinated by and skilled in the new technology, yet reluctant to settle in any one place.

For five years after 1863, Edison was part of this traveling community, working in many parts of the country. As an expert telegrapher, with a sending speed of 45 words a minute, he was never short of a job. But in 1868, Edison's hearing began to fail. It is unclear why this happened, though the condition may have started in boyhood. He never went completely deaf and was able, with some difficulty, to take part in quiet conversations. But he was forced to give up working as a telegrapher.

Morse's early telegraph machine. It was on this that the first telegraph message was sent from Washington D.C. to Baltimore in 1844, asking, "What hath God wrought [What has God made]?"

above, right). Five magnetized needles were fixed on a panel marked with all the letters of the alphabet. When an electric impulse was sent down the wire, it deflected two of the needles to spell out a message.

THE MORSE CODE

The true founder of the electric telegraph industry was Samuel Morse (1791–1872). After graduating from Yale in 1810, Morse went to England to study art. It was not until the 1830s that he became interested in electricity. Morse replaced letters with an alphabetic code in which each letter was represented by one or more dots (.), one or more dashes (–), or a combination of both. This is still known as the Morse Code.

INVENTING FOR THE PEOPLE

The late19th and early 20th centuries saw a flurry of inventions that would revolutionize the lives of ordinary people. More than 1,000 inventions were patented by Edison himself; other groundbreaking ideas of the period included the telephone, patented in 1876 by the Scottish-born American inventor Alexander Graham Bell (1847-1922), and the first successful gasoline-engined automobile, built in 1885 by the German engineer Karl Friedrich Benz (1844-1929).

It was vital to the success of these new products that people wanted to buy them, but it was just as important that they could afford them. New inventions were often expensive when first put on the market; using mass production techniques, their manufacturing costs could be reduced to bring them within the reach of what most people could afford. Instead of being individually handcrafted, these new commercial products were built in factories from standardized parts. Work was divided into simple, individual tasks, and specialized machinery and equipment often replaced humans. In 1903 the creation of a glass-blowing machine to replace human glass-blowers meant that one man could produce 1,250 light bulbs an hour. This breakthrough ensured the success of Edison's incandescent light bulb (see pages 28-29).

The Assembly Line

A further aid to lowering production costs was the assembly line, introduced in 1913 by American industrialist Henry Ford (1863-1947). Ford had seen the technique used in slaughterhouses, but he applied it to the production of automobiles in the Ford Motor Company plant in Detroit, Michigan. An automobile chassis was carried on a moving conveyor belt at slow speed; workers standing along the belt added parts as it passed by. In the past, one automobile had taken 12.5 hours to assemble; now it took just 1.5 hours. Using this method Ford produced his famous Model T car, known as the Tin Lizzie; by 1915 he had sold more than a million of them in the United States alone.

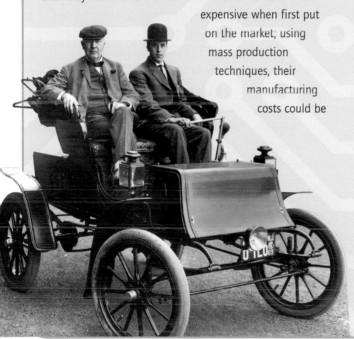

This picture (left) from 1910 shows Thomas Edison and his son in an electric automobile.

WORKING AS A FREELANCE INVENTOR

In 1869 Edison decided instead to become a freelance inventor. Not surprisingly, his first inventions were connected with telegraphy. Edison's Universal Stock Printer was a "stock ticker," a machine that was used for printing out the changing prices on the Stock Exchange. Western Union paid him a handsome sum of money for the machine.

He then went on to develop the duplex, a device that doubled the capacity of a single telegraph wire by allowing operators to send messages in both directions at the same time. In 1874 Edison invented the quadruplex, which allowed the transmission of two messages each way. Now every mile of expensive wire was able to do the work of four miles. Railroad baron Jay Gould (1836-1892) paid Edison more than $100,000 for the rights to this invention, despite Western Union's prior claims to it. This was to involve Edison in years of litigation. But by now his inventive mind was beginning to turn in other directions.

AN EFFICIENT SYSTEM

In 1878 Edison established the Electric Light Company with the purpose of finding a safe, cheap alternative to gaslighting. To do this, he had to find a suitable circuit. If a series circuit (see below) was used, all the lights on the system would either be on or off at the same time. In this system, too, the failure of one light bulb would cause the whole circuit to fail.

Edison proposed to connect his lights in a parallel circuit by subdividing the current to run through two different wires. This could be done only by using a high-resistance system. Resistance is the opposition to the flow of current presented by the various parts of a circuit, and is measured in ohms. Current traveling through a low-resistance system generates a lot of heat, and requires thick, expensive copper cable to power an entire city district. By contrast, a high-resistance system restricts the volume of the current. It is more efficient because less current generates less heat. But a high-resistance light bulb had not yet been invented for this system—obliging Edison to begin his search.

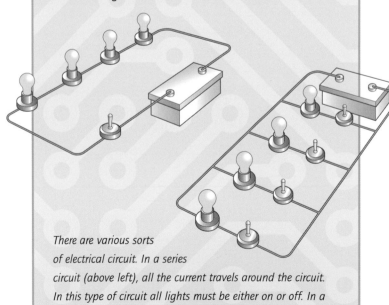

There are various sorts of electrical circuit. In a series circuit (above left), all the current travels around the circuit. In this type of circuit all lights must be either on or off. In a parallel circuit (above right), the current divides so that only a portion of it runs through each part of the circuit. The lights are controlled individually by switches.

THE SEARCH FOR EFFECTIVE LIGHT BULBS

In 1876 Edison established a laboratory and machine shop in the rural environs of Newark, New Jersey. With two associates, Charles Batchelor, a master mechanic and draftsman, and John Kruesi, a Swiss-born machinist, he began working on a wide range of experiments. One area of investigation that took his interest was electric lighting. In 1808 the English scientist Humphry Davy (1778–1829) had connected the wires from a battery to two carbon rods and noted that "a bright spark was produced and more than half the volume of the charcoal became ignited to whiteness." This was the arc lamp. But although arc lighting replaced gas lighting in some areas, it had limited uses. The light was so bright that it was more suitable for a lighthouse than a home. It was also very hot, expensive to produce, needed regular adjustment, and smelled unpleasant.

A better option was the incandescent lamp, in which light is produced by heating a thin wire. When an electric current is passed through a filament it heats up and emits light. But whatever material was used for the filament, it completely burned away (oxidized) when mixed with oxygen in the air. The obvious answer was to enclose the filament in a glass globe from which the air had been pumped out. However, in the absence of an efficient vacuum pump, this was not an easy task. Nor was it obvious which material would make a cheap and long-lasting filament.

The first choice was carbon, the element with the highest melting point, 6,422°F (3,550°C). In 1877 Edison tested charred (carbonized) paper, but found that it burned up too quickly. Edison then turned to the metal platinum, which has a melting point of 3,222°F (1,772°C). However it failed to produce a satisfactory light, and in any case was extremely expensive. Edison's search for a suitable filament revealed many of his great qualities: determination, persistence, ingenuity, and incredibly hard work. He often worked days and nights at a stretch, and expected his assistants to do the same. Sometimes he took brief naps on a lab bench before carrying on. In all he tested more than 1,600 materials. Edison regarded the painstaking work as a valuable exercise: "I have not failed," he remarked of the tests. "I have just found 10,000 ways that won't work."

This portrait of Thomas Edison depicts him surrounded by books and laboratory apparatus, and examining his incandescent light bulb. The engraving (right) shows the bulb in detail. Choosing the right filament and creating an effective vacuum in the bulb were crucial to its success.

THOMAS ALVA EDISON

A BREAKTHROUGH AT LAST

The first real progress came when Edison heard that a much better vacuum pump was available. It had been invented in 1852 by the German chemist Herman Sprengel (1834–1906). Use of the much more efficient Sprengel pump allowed Edison to consider carbon filaments again. This proved to be a messy and time-consuming business. He would start with some cotton threads, pack them with powdered carbon, heat them in a furnace, and mold them with soot. The filament would then be taken to a glass-blower who sealed it in a globe using the new vacuum pump. The filaments were drawn extremely fine, so they were very prone to breaking.

In October 1879 Edison noted that a carbon filament had worked for 13.5 hours. A few days later he recorded a filament that had burned for 170 hours, and on November 1 applied for a patent for a carbon-filament lamp, and began to produce his new bulb in quantity. He later found carbonized (charred) bamboo to be better as a filament. In 1882 Edison produced 100,000 bulbs in a single year; within 20 years he was selling 45 million a year.

Improvements were gradually made to the light bulb. The invention of a glass-blowing machine in 1903 meant that large quantities of light bulbs could be produced quickly, and an inert gas such as argon was used in the bulb to lengthen the life of the filament. In 1911 the carbon filament was replaced by one of tungsten. Tungsten can be drawn into thin wires; a 7-inch length no thicker than a pencil lead can make 100 miles of filament. Tungsten also produces a white light rather than the yellow light of the carbon filament.

ELECTRICITY FOR ALL

In 1882 Edison opened an electricity generating station in New York City. By the close of the following year he had acquired 431 customers and was supplying power to more than 2,000 lamps. At the same time Edison and his English partner, the physicist Joseph Swan (1828–1914), opened a power station in London, England. The age of electricity had arrived. At first the new power seemed very strange to customers used to gas, and electricity did not become common in homes for some years. By 1914 only about 10 percent of

MOVING PICTURES

By the end of the 19th century experimentation with moving photography was well under way. An early pioneer was Eadweard Muybridge (1830–1904), who succeeded in taking a series of action photographs of a trotting horse; using paper film, Frenchman Étienne-Jules Marey (1830–1904) was able to reduce exposure time to thousandths of a second to photograph insects in flight.

In 1888 George Eastman (1854–1932) developed light-sensitive celluloid roll film suitable for taking moving pictures, and by 1891 William Dickson, one of Edison's employees, had built a camera, the Kinetograph, to use it, together with a device for viewing the film, called the Kinetoscope. Public viewing parlors sprang up everywhere, but the films only lasted about a minute, and they could only be viewed by one person at a time peering through a hole in a wooden box.

Meanwhile the French Lumière brothers, Auguste (1862–1954) and Louis (1864–1948), had built a combined camera, printer, and projector called the Cinématographe. This projected films onto a large screen, so lots of people could view them at the same time. It had its first public demonstration in Paris on December 28, 1895, and became a huge popular success. Edison was forced to buy the rights to a film projector he called the Vitascope in order to compete with them.

American homes had electricity, and in other countries the figure was lower. In the 19th century it was still mainly used for public lighting, gradually replacing gas lamps in streets, factories, theaters, and stores. Later it was used to power transportation; in 1903 the first electric tram service came into service in London.

Electricity was also adopted as a method of executing convicted criminals. Edison did not want the public to think of his power supply when they thought of the electric chair, so he proposed that the electricity system of his biggest rival, George Westinghouse (1846–1914), should be used. When the first execution by electricity was performed in 1890, the word

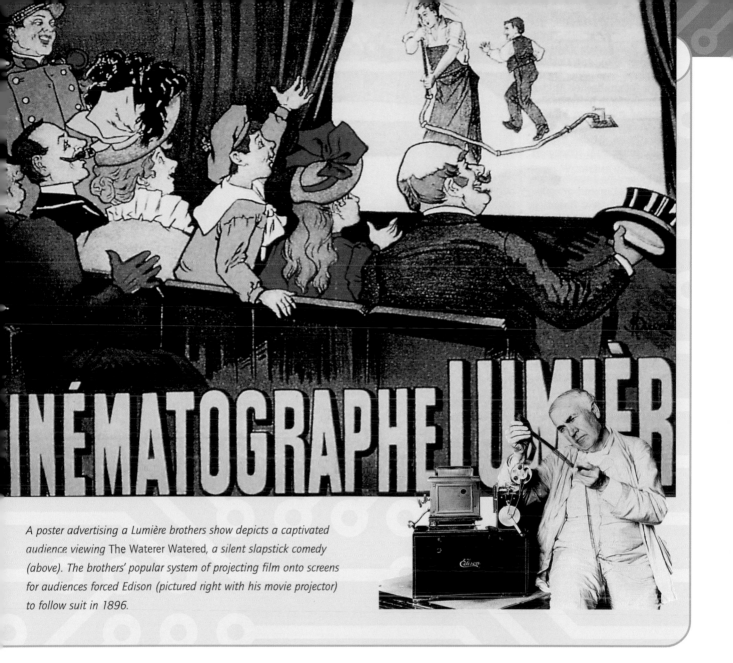

A poster advertising a Lumière brothers show depicts a captivated audience viewing The Waterer Watered, *a silent slapstick comedy (above). The brothers' popular system of projecting film onto screens for audiences forced Edison (pictured right with his movie projector) to follow suit in 1896.*

"electrocution" had not been invented, and one of Edison's supporters suggested that the process should be known as being "westinghoused."

THE PHONOGRAPH

The name of Edison will ever be associated with the phonograph, a machine for recording sound that he began developing as early as 1877. Inventors before Edison had suggested that sounds, if they could be graphically recorded, would produce distinct shapes. Edison set out to see if he could do this. He used a carbon transmitter with a stylus tip to make indentations in a strip of paraffined paper. When

Joseph Swan
1828–1914

Joseph Swan was born in England. He became an apprentice to a druggist, and then worked for a manufacturing chemist. In 1871 he invented a new type of photographic plate, and developed bromide paper for making photographic prints. By 1860 Swann had made a carbon-filament lamp. It was not until 1880 that he developed a practical light bulb, applying for a patent while also setting up the Swan Electric Company. Swan's patent was virtually identical to Edison's. They decided to merge in 1883.

George Westinghouse
1846–1914

George Westinghouse was an American engineer and inventor. He learned his trade making and maintaining agricultural machinery, and then served in the Union Army during the Civil War (1861–65) and later as an engineer in the U.S. Navy.

In 1865 he invented a device for getting derailed railroad cars back onto the rails, and three years later he produced a cast-steel "frog" for railroad switches (the frog is the V-shaped piece where the rails fork). In 1872 Westinghouse perfected his most famous invention, a brake for railroad vehicles that used compressed air generated by the locomotive. Within 20 years air brakes were compulsory on all trains in the United States.

In 1886 he founded the Westinghouse Electric Company, and championed the use of high-voltage alternating current (AC) for the distribution of electric power. His system won favor over the direct-current (DC) distribution introduced by Edison, and eventually received nationwide acceptance.

letters, the public used the phonograph almost entirely to play recorded music. However, the phonograph was soon overtaken in popularity by the superior disk gramophone, invented in 1888 by German-born American Emile Berliner (1851–1929).

THE LIGHTS GO OUT

By 1886 Edison had set up a laboratory in West Orange, New Jersey, as a scientific research facility. There he continued to develop the phonograph, and laid the foundations of the motion picture industry. He invented an alkaline storage battery that was used in submarines, and designed a battery for use on Ford's Model T car. During the late 1880s and early 1890s he became involved in a disastrous magnetic ore-mining venture, which he financed using most of his General Electric Company shares. He spent the years of World War I (1914–18) chairing a scientific advisory committee, and finding ways of detecting torpedoes.

Edison carried on working well into his eighties. A huge self-publicist, ever since the 1870s he had been one of the best-known people in the world. On the announcement of his death in 1931 the lights of America were extinguished for one minute in his honor.

the paper was pulled back beneath the stylus, he found that a vague series of sounds were generated. In other words, he had managed to record sound as graphical marks and play it back. His next model used a sheet of grooved tinfoil wrapped around a horizontal cylinder.

Edison demonstrated his phonograph ("soundwriter") in December 1877. It had three main parts: a cone-shaped speaking tube, a hand-cranked cylinder covered with tinfoil, and a playback device. Speaking into the tube caused a diaphragm (a very thin disk) to vibrate. A needle connected to the diaphragm left a characteristic pattern of grooves on the foil as the crank slowly rotated it. When Edison rewound the cylinder to its original position and played it back, his voice was heard emerging faintly from the tube as he recited "Mary had a little lamb..."

Improvements soon followed. An electric motor was added, a funnel amplified the sound, and wax replaced the original tinfoil. Although Edison had imagined the machine would be used by business people for dictating

This photograph of great inventors shows Edison (far left), Henry Ford (second from right), and Harvey Firestone (1868–1938), manufacturer of the pneumatic tire (far right). An early Edison phonograph with a hand-cranked cylinder (below).

SCIENTIFIC BACKGROUND

Before 1850

Italian physicist Alessandro Volta (1745–1827) invents the electric battery

French engineer Claude Chappe (1763–1805) invents a hand-operated telegraph system

Samuel Morse (1791–1872) invents the Morse Code

1860 English chemist Joseph Swan (1828–1914) invents a carbon-filament electric lamp

1866 The first underwater telegraph cable is installed across the Atlantic Ocean between Britain and the United States

1868 Edison invents an electric vote-recording machine

1876 Scots-born American inventor Alexander Graham Bell (1847–1922) patents the telephone

1877 Edison demonstrates his phonograph

1879 Edison invents the electric light bulb

1888 American inventor George Eastman (1854–1932) develops light-sensitive celluloid roll film suitable for moving pictures

1895 The French Lumière brothers, Auguste (1862–1954) and Louis (1864–1948), mount the first public film show using their Cinématographe

1901 Italian physicist and inventor Guglielmo Marconi (1874–1937) transmits radio signals across the Atlantic

1903 The Wright Brothers, Orville (1871–1948) and Wilbur (1867–1912), make the first controlled flight in a heavier-than-air machine

1912 Edison produces the first talking motion pictures

1913 American industrialist Henry Ford (1863–1947) introduces the assembly line to produce his Model T car

1926 English physicist Edward Appleton (1892–1965) discovers the "Appleton layer" of the Earth's atmosphere, which reflects radio waves to make distant communication possible

After 1940

1952 The first commercially viable video recorder is demonstrated in the United States

1982 The first compact disk players are launched by Sony in Japan

---

1850 **1870** **1900** **1920**

POLITICAL AND CULTURAL BACKGROUND

1851 American novelist Herman Melville (1819–1891) completes his classic tale, *Moby Dick*

1855 Alexander II (1818–1881) succeeds to the Russian throne and carries out a series of reforms, including freeing of serfs (slaves) in 1861

1861 Decades of friction over trade, slavery, and the rights of individual states lead to the outbreak of the American Civil War (1861–65)

1871 American artist James Whistler (1834–1903) completes *Arrangement in Gray and Black No. 1*, better known as "Whistler's Mother"

1876 New York's Central Park is completed

1890–91 American architect Louis Sullivan (1856–1924) designs the Wainwright Building in St. Louis, Missouri, one of the earliest skyscrapers

1898 The Spanish-American War marks the end of Spain's imperial power and leads to the fall of the Spanish monarchy three years later

1903 The Tour de France is launched by a French newspaper owner as a publicity stunt; it will become the most famous cycling race in the world

1909 American director D. W. Griffith (1875–1948) creates one of Hollywood's first stars in Mary Pickford, born Gladys Smith (1892–1979), who becomes known as "the world's sweetheart"

1920 The Government of Ireland Act divides Ireland into the six counties of the north and 26 of the south, with separate parliaments for each

ALEXANDER GRAHAM BELL

1847–1922

"There cannot be mental atrophy [degeneration] in any person who continues to observe, to remember what he observes, and to seek answers for his unceasing hows and whys about things."

Alexander Graham Bell

BEST KNOWN FOR INVENTING THE TELEPHONE—WHICH TRANSFORMED COMMUNICATIONS WORLDWIDE—ALEXANDER GRAHAM BELL ALSO HELPED TO DEVELOP MANY OTHER IDEAS, SUCH AS THE ELECTRIC TELEGRAPH, A "PHOTOPHONE," HYDROFOILS, AND AIRPLANES.

Alexander Graham Bell's grandfather taught elocution (the technique of clear speaking) in London, while his father, Melville Bell, invented a system of writing down speech that he called "Visible Speech." Unlike modern methods that indicate sounds (phonetics), Melville Bell used diagrams to show the positions of the tongue, teeth, and lips during speech. This was intended to make it particularly suitable for teaching deaf people to speak. Alexander also would later direct his work to helping deaf people.

A FRESH START

Alexander was born in Edinburgh, Scotland, the second of three sons. He attended school on and off until he was 14, but his education was largely gained at home. After spending a year in London in 1862, Alexander returned to Scotland and taught music and elocution at Weston House Academy in Elgin; he later taught in Bath, England.

In 1868 he moved to London, and began work as his father's assistant. In 1870 his older brother Melville died, aged 25, of tuberculosis which had killed his younger brother two years previously; shocked and distressed by the loss of both his brothers, Alexander

The "phonautograph," or sound writer, was an early Bell invention. The device recorded speech by making a wavy line on the smoked glass below the receiver. Deaf people were intended to imitate the patterns made by hearing speakers, and so improve their own speech.

KEY DATES

1870 The family emigrates to Canada

1871 Teaches deaf people in Boston, Massachusetts

1873 Appointed professor of vocal physiology at Boston University

1875 Obtains patent for first transmission of sound by telephone

1877 Bell Telephone Company established; marries Mabel Hubbard

1878 Daughter Elsie May is born

1880 Daughter Marian (Daisy) is born; Volta Laboratory set up

1886 Establishes Volta Bureau as center of study into deafness

1897 Elected president of the National Geographic Society

1915 Takes part in opening of first transcontinental telephone line

This contemporary print shows Bell demonstrating his best-known invention, the telephone. The first private telephone was installed in a house in Boston, Massachusetts, on April 4, 1877.

himself became sick. He and his parents emigrated to Canada, which was thought to be a particularly healthy place to live. While Alexander recovered, Melville Bell began at once to lecture on his Visible Speech system.

The Boston School for the Deaf was interested in adopting the system, and in 1871 the staff there invited Melville Bell to show them how it worked. He sent Alexander instead, who quickly established a practice in Boston working with deaf people, and by 1873 had been appointed professor of vocal physiology at Boston University.

HELP FOR THE DEAF

Much of Bell's early experimental work concerned developing devices to help deaf people to communicate. He first tried to make what he called a "phonautograph," which aimed to convert speech into written sound patterns. In this way deaf people could easily check their own speech. In the course of developing his new machine, Bell experimented with various types of membrane, including a real human eardrum, in order to try to imitate the way it worked. The eardrum is a thin, semitransparent, pliable structure: how, he wondered, could such a membrane move the solid bones of the inner ear? If a thin membrane could do such heavy work, might it not also respond to sound waves by somehow modifying the flow of an electric current?

Initial experiments were unsuccessful, however. Bell was able to take his work further only because Gardiner Greene Hubbard, a wealthy Boston attorney who had interests in the electric telegraph, now stepped in with an offer to finance him. Hubbard's daughter Mabel had been made deaf at the age of five by an attack of scarlet fever. She was a pupil of Bell's, and Hubbard was so impressed by his efforts on her behalf that he agreed to back him. Mabel later (in 1877) became Bell's wife.

SENDING WORDS WITH ELECTRICITY

Bell did not set out to invent the telephone. He had originally begun trying to develop a "harmonic" or "multiple telegraph," a device that could receive several telegraph messages at once. In 1874 he took on as an assistant a young mechanic and model-maker called

Thomas Augustus Watson
1854-1934

Bell first met Watson in 1874 when he was recommended to him as an assistant. They worked together for several years, developing the telephone, and Watson became a shareholder in the original Bell company.

After leaving Bell in 1881 Watson tried farming before setting up as a shipbuilder. From 1896 to 1904 Watson's Fore River Ship and Engine Company at Massachusetts built vessels including battleships and schooners. In 1904 he trained at the Massachusetts Institute of Technology as a geologist. He spent some time unsuccessfully searching California and Alaska for something of value to mine.

Watson became an actor at the age of 54 and took on roles in plays by William Shakespeare (1564–1616) at Stratford-on-Avon, England. In 1912 he returned to the United States. He spent the rest of his life in amateur dramatics, writing his autobiography, *Exploring Life* (1926), and giving interviews about his time with Bell.

Thomas Watson (1854–1934). Together they worked on trying to develop another idea of Bell's: a device that would be able to transmit speech using electricity.

The principles behind Bell's and all other work in this field derive from the researches of Danish physicist Hans Christian Oersted (1777–1851) and English chemist and physicist Michael Faraday (1791–1867). In 1820 Oersted discovered that, if he passed an electric current through a wire, it generated a magnetic field around it. In 1831 Faraday proved that disturbances in this magnetic field can generate an electric current, whose strength depends on how much the magnetic field is disturbed. This is known as "induction;" it produces an "induced" current.

A tuning fork consists of two metal prongs. When struck, they vibrate to produce a note of an exact pitch. Bell linked a tuning fork to an electromagnet. The strength of the current induced by the electromagnet depended on the pitch of the vibrating tuning fork. This current could then flow through a wire to a second electromagnet and produce in a second tuning fork the same note as the first. Bell hoped that several forks tuned to different frequencies might be used to send different messages at the same time.

The breakthrough came in June 1875, when Watson was in one room and Bell in another. Vibrating reeds had taken the place of tuning forks in their device. One of the reeds had stopped vibrating and Watson gave it a tap. In a distant room Bell heard a loud twang—sound had been transmitted. On February 14, 1876, Bell filed a telephone patent application at the United States Patent Office, giving him the right to be the only person to make and sell his invention for a limited time. Just a few hours later, another patent for a telephone was filed from a rival, Elisha Gray (1835–1901). This would lead to the first of many challenges to Bell's patent (see box page 39). However, on March 7, the Patent Office issued the patent to Bell for "the method of, and apparatus for, transmitting vocal or other sound telegraphically...by causing electrical undulations..."

Bell's notebook entry of March 10, 1876 describes the exciting events of the day, as Watson took his place in one room with the "Receiving Instrument," and Bell

Telephone wires are in abundance in this photograph of the commercial district of Dallas, Texas, in 1908 (left). Bell using an early model of the telephone (below).

In Bell's early telephone, the speaker talks into a cone (below, left side). A membrane in the narrow end vibrates in response to sound, in turn vibrating an electromagnet. The second vibration causes a variable electric current to flow along a wire to the receiver's end (pointed end at right). These vibrations reproduce speech sounds.

took up position in another room next to the "Transmitting Instrument." Bell shouted into the transmitter, "Mr Watson—Come here—I want to see you," and his notebook records what happened next. "To my delight he came and declared that he had heard and understood what I said. We then changed places.... The sentence, 'Mr Bell do you understand what I say? Do—you—un—der—stand—what—I—say?' came quite clearly...." The new invention stole the show at the 1876 Centennial Exhibition in Philadelphia.

Bell devoted a great deal of his later years to designing flying machines, such as The Bell Cygnet II (right). It had 5,000 tetrahedral cells, but flight tests proved unsuccessful.

NEW PROJECTS

Bell continued to work on other methods of communication. His next project was the "photophone," or light-sounder. In the early 1870s it had been discovered that the electrical resistance of the element selenium varied with the intensity of the light falling on it. Bell thought he could see in this a way to use a beam of light to transmit speech. A speaker's voice made a beam of light vibrate. The vibrating light beam was directed onto a piece of selenium, altering its resistance and thereby producing a varying electric current that could be turned back into sound.

Bell became very excited by this idea and he achieved some initial success in developing it. His enthusiasm was not shared by investors, though, who were more interested in putting money into the new telephone system.

Bell's curiosity had already led him onto a range of other projects. In 1901 he invented the tetrahedral kite—a kite with four triangular sides. This proved to be a very successful design, and he built gigantic versions, capable of carrying people. With four colleagues, and funding from his wife Mabel, in 1907 he formed the Aerial Experiment Association (AEA). On February 23, 1909, the AEA's biplane, the Silver Dart, was the first heavier-than-air craft to fly in Canada.

A sketch of Bell's photophone shows the soundwaves from the speaker being converted into light. The vibrating light beam is directed onto a piece of selenium, which produces an electric current that turns the light back into sound.

WHOSE IDEA WAS IT ANYWAY?

Bell's offer to sell his patents to the Western Union telegraph company in 1876 was rejected. So Bell assigned the patents to his father-in-law, Gardiner Hubbard. By the time the Bell Telephone Company had been established in 1877, the first of many legal challenges had been issued against Bell.

In the United States the rights to inventions go to whoever first had the idea. Thus there can be a tendency in the United States for unknown inventors to "discover" old notebooks in order to prove they were first to come up with the device.

Over a period of 18 years there were some 600 challenges to Bell's patents. Some of these were fraudulent. Others were little more than blackmail, threatening endless nuisance and lawsuits unless

the petitioner was paid off. However, the most famous of the lawsuits involving Bell's telephone was launched by the Bell Telephone Company against Western Union and Elisha Gray, who had filed a rival patent. The two sides finally reached an agreement, and *The Boston Daily Advertiser* of October 25, 1879 reported that "the rival and conflicting interests in the various telephone patents have at last been harmonized, and Professor Bell is master of the field..."

Patently Profitable

There was good reason for people to want to own Bell's patents. As *The Boston Daily Advertiser* noted, "The Bell telephone has a future of fame and fortune in store for

it not surpassed by any of the great discoveries of our time." The growth of the telephone business was indeed phenomenal. As early as 1878 the first telephone exchange switchboard was operating in New Haven, Connecticut. By the end of the century there were more than a million phones in the United States, a figure that had grown to 186 million a century later. The challenges continued throughout the lifetime of the patents, but Bell won every case. By 1883 the stock he held in the companies that owned his patents had made him a millionaire.

The fashion for patenting strange inventions inspired this 1885 cartoon showing the "patent steam arm for newly elected presidents during the public hand-shaking season in Washington."

Bell also tried to develop a reliable and efficient hydrofoil craft. A hydrofoil is a boat that has "wings" placed under the hull that are connected to the boat by vertical spars. When the boat accelerates the wings develop "lift" and help raise the hull out of the water. This reduces drag on the hull and so allows the boat to travel much faster than a normal craft. In 1906 Bell began work on his "heavier-than-water" machine. His first model, the HD-1, had encouraging results in tests, reaching a speed of 50 mph (80.4 kmh) before breaking up. Bell continued to work on and off on the project for the best part of a decade. When the United States entered World War I in 1917 Bell tried to interest the navy in his new model, HD-4. Trials went well, and the hydrofoil reached a top speed of 54 mph (87 kmh). Although the Navy thought that the craft was too fragile for active service, the HD-4 set a world marine speed record that would not be broken until 1963.

PERSONAL INTEREST

A more personal quest was Bell's attempt to develop a "vacuum jacket." His baby son, Edward, had died in 1881 of breathing problems, and Bell wanted to design a jacket that would help people breathe by reducing the air pressure around the body. Once that had been done, atmospheric pressure forced air through the patient's mouth and into the lungs. This type of device would later—as the "iron lung"—be widely used to help patients with the infectious viral disease polio.

Bell died on August 2, 1922. As he told a reporter a few months earlier, he had continued trying to "seek answers for his unceasing hows and whys about things."

PRIZES AND PATRONAGE

Bell was an enthusiastic patron. In 1880 he was awarded the Volta Prize by the French government for his invention of the telephone; he used the prize money to set up the Volta Laboratory for scientific research in Washington, D.C. Bell also co-funded publication of *Science*, later the official journal of the American Association for the Advancement of Science. As president of the National Geographic Society, he was convinced that pictures were the best means of showing the world to people who could not travel, and helped develop the society's journal into the visual feast that became famous worldwide.

Bell's lifelong interest in helping the deaf led him to set up the Volta Bureau as a center for studies on the subject, and to found the American Association to Promote the Teaching of Speech to the Deaf (renamed the Alexander Graham Bell Association for the Deaf in 1956). In 1887 he met Helen Keller (1880–1968). She

The transistor, developed in 1947, is perhaps the most important advance to have emerged from the Bell Lab so far. It was invented by (from left to right) William Shockley (1910–1989), Walter Brattain (1902–1987), and John Bardeen (1908–1991). They received the 1956 Nobel Prize for physics for their work.

had become blind and deaf at 19 months old, and Bell found a teacher who was able to teach her to speak. In 1893 the 13-year-old Keller (later to become a famous writer and lecturer) ceremonially opened the new Volta Bureau building.

After his death, Bell's name was given to one of the world's most important scientific institutions, the Bell Laboratories. Known more familiarly as the Bell Lab, it was founded in 1925 with a staff of 3,000 and located in Murray Hill, New Jersey. By 1983 the Bell Lab had been granted 20,000 patents and its staff had been awarded seven Nobel prizes.

Before 1870

Danish physicist Hans Christian Oersted (1777–1851) shows that an electric current produces a magnetic field

English physicist Michael Faraday (1791–1867) induces electric current by disrupting a magnetic field

American inventor Samuel Morse (1791–1872) patents the telegraph

1875 In Boston, Massachusetts, Bell and his assistant Thomas A. Watson (1854–1934) transmit sound electronically

1876 Bell sends the first long-distance telephone message 8 miles (13 km) from Paris, Ontario, to Brantford, Ontario

1880 In his laboratories at Baddeck Bay, Nova Scotia, Bell sends the first wireless telephone message by "photophone" (lightphone)

1881 Bell designs the vacuum jacket, a forerunner of the iron lung

1886 Bell sets up the Volta Bureau in Washington D.C. for research to help the deaf

1891 The American scientist and engineer Samuel Langley (1834–1906) begins work with Bell on problems of flight

1896 Italian physicist Guglielmo Marconi (1874–1937) obtains a patent to use electromagnetic waves "for the purpose of wireless telegraphy"

1901 Marconi makes the first transAtlantic radio transmission

1903 Brothers Orville (1871–1948) and Wilbur Wright (1867–1912) fly the first piloted airplane

1906 Bell begins work on hydrofoil speed boats

1909 French aviator Louis Blériot (1872–1936) flies from France to England

After 1910

1956 The first transAtlantic telephone cables are laid

1962 Telstar is the first communications satellite to be launched

---

1870   **1880**   **1890**   **1900**

1873 New York's first streetcar goes into operation

1876 General George Custer (1839–1876) leads 264 men of the U.S. 7th Cavalry to their death at the hands of Sioux warriors in "Custer's Last Stand," on the Little Bighorn river in Montana

1883 American showman William Frederick "Buffalo Bill" Cody (1846–1917) begins a tour of the United States and Europe with his Wild West Show

1884 In Barcelona, Spain, work begins on the ornate and fantastical Sagrada Familia church, designed by Antonio Gaudí (1852–1926); it is still under construction today

1890 At Wounded Knee Creek, South Dakota, the U.S. 7th Cavalry massacre 200 Sioux men, women, and children

1895 In Germany, Rudolf Diesel (1858–1913) invents the diesel engine

1898 In the Spanish-American War, the United States acquires Puerto Rico, Guam, and the Philippines, and Cuba wins its independence from Spain

1903 The first baseball World Series takes place in the United States

1911 In China the Kuomintang "Revolutionary Alliance," under the leadership of Sun Yat-Sen (1866–1925) depose the last ruler of the Qing dynasty, the child emperor Pu Yi (1906–1967), and form a republic

FRITZ HABER

1868–1934

"The production of nitrogen is vital to the progress of civilized humanity...it is the chemist who must come to the rescue..."

William Crookes, British scientist
(1813–1919)

Fritz Haber was born in Breslau, Silesia in 1868, to a German-Jewish family. Silesia was then part of Prussia. Three years later Prussia became part of the newly formed German empire, or Second Reich. Haber's father was a trader in natural dyes, and after studying at the German universities of Berlin and Heidelberg, and at Zurich in Switzerland, Haber joined the family business as a salesman. However, he disagreed with his father over the future of synthetic dyes (dyes produced artificially through a chemical reaction) and left the company.

Haber then secured a post in the Department of Chemical and Fuel Technology at the Karlsruhe Technical University in Germany. His work at Karlsruhe would have two dramatically different effects. On the one hand it would save the world from starvation. On the other, it would create a way of killing and disabling many thousands of people quickly and efficiently.

THE NEED FOR NITRATES

In 1840 German chemist Justus von Liebig (1803–1873) concluded that among the "foods" needed by plants for healthy growth were nitrogen and potassium. He thought that plants got nitrogen from the air. In fact, they absorb nutrients from the soil. When land is intensively farmed year after year, unless nutrients are returned to the soil via fertilizers, plant yields get lower. Traditional farming used animal manure as a fertilizer, but the world's population was rapidly growing at the end of the 19th century, demanding an ever-increasing food supply. More and more land was coming into production, so huge amounts of fertilizer were needed. The question was, where could supplies be found?

For a time Chile saltpeter (sodium nitrate) provided the answer. But these deposits were running out. At the start of the 20th century scientists warned that a chemical solution must be found to the problem.

ARTIFICIAL DYES

Haber had warned his father that trade in natural dyes was doomed. He was soon proved to be right. Before the 1850s, dyes came from plants or animals. Natural dyes included blue indigo and red alizarin (from plants), crimson cochineal (from an insect), and Tyrian purple (from a Mediterranean shellfish). Tyrian purple was so rare and expensive that only emperors could afford to have their clothes dyed with it.

In 1856 an English chemistry student named William Perkin (1838–1907) made the first synthetic dye. He was trying to make the antimalaria drug quinine from a coal tar product called aniline. Instead, he produced the purple dye "mauve," the first of many aniline dyes. In 1868 Perkin made synthetic alizarin. In 1879 the German chemist Johann von Baeyer (1835–1917) synthesized indigo, an achievement for which he was awarded the 1905 Nobel Prize for chemistry. With a few changes to the chemical structure of indigo, von Beyer was able to produce Tyrian purple. Now everyone could afford "the emperors' color," and within 25 years the producers and importers of natural dyes had been put out of business.

Perfumes and Potions

The perfume industry—like the dye industry—had previously relied on natural products from plants and animals. Coumarin was one of these products, a white vanilla-scented solid that occurs in beans of the tonka tree, native to South America. Perkin found a way of synthesizing it. Coumarin was the first artificial perfume, and led to the creation of a synthetic perfume industry. Later, doctors found medical uses for coumarin in the

A late 19th-century print depicts women showing off their multicolored costumes. The manufacture of synthetic dyes meant that colored clothes became much more affordable.

treatment of blood diseases. It prevents the blood from clotting, and its modern synthetic derivative, warfarin, is still used for this purpose—and as a rat poison.

The issue was particularly serious in Germany. In the years leading up to World War I (1914–18), it was concentrating its resources on becoming a leading world power. Nitrates (nitrogen-containing salts) were not only essential for fertilizers, they were also a vital component in many explosives. Leading figures in Germany soon realized that, in the event of a major war, German ports would be blockaded to cut off fresh supplies of nitrates. Nitrates could be recovered from ammonia, a compound of nitrogen and hydrogen, but

KEY DATES

1908	Appointed professor of chemistry at Karlsruhe Technical University
1911	Becomes director of the Kaiser Wilhelm Institute for Chemistry, Berlin
1916	Appointed director of the chemical warfare service
1918	Awarded Nobel Prize for Chemistry

ammonia was very expensive to make. It was obvious that other sources would need to be found.

What was needed was a way of making ammonia by synthesizing it from nitrogen in the atmosphere and hydrogen extracted from coal gas. Earlier attempts to make nitrogen react with hydrogen using an electric spark failed when it was found that a temperature of up to 3,000°C (5,432°F) was needed. When chemists cannot get a desired chemical reaction, they often resort to the use of catalysts. A catalyst is a substance whose presence can speed up a chemical reaction. The catalyst itself is not used up during the reaction.

Haber therefore tried to combine nitrogen and hydrogen using a suitable catalyst. Eventually in 1903 he succeeded in combining nitrogen and hydrogen at a temperature of 1,000°C (1,832°F) using an iron catalyst. The yields, however, were too small to be commercially useful. A colleague, Walther Nernst (1864–1941), pointed out that increasing the pressure might help the reaction, and after further calculation Haber worked out how much extra pressure would be needed to get a productive reaction.

During the Haber-Bosch process nitrogen from liquefied air reacts with hydrogen from coal gas at very high temperatures and pressure. This produces ammonia gas, which is condensed to produce liquid ammonia.

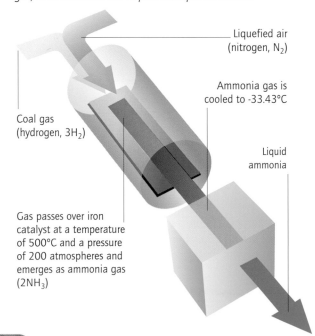

Liquefied air
(nitrogen, N_2)

Ammonia gas is cooled to -33.43°C

Coal gas
(hydrogen, $3H_2$)

Liquid ammonia

Gas passes over iron catalyst at a temperature of 500°C and a pressure of 200 atmospheres and emerges as ammonia gas ($2NH_3$)

POISONING THE ENEMY

Soon after the outbreak of World War I in 1914, Haber became head of the chemical warfare division of the German government. His task was to work out how poisonous gases could be used to disable or kill the enemy without harming advancing German forces. In 1914 Haber had witnessed an unsuccessful test of artillery shells filled with tear gas (a synthetic compound that irritates the eye, causing temporary blindness). Because it was very light, it dispersed too quickly, Haber proposed that chlorine, a poisonous, choking gas that is heavier than air, would be more effective.

Germany had signed the 1899 Hague Convention banning such weapons. However, the German High Command argued that this only banned the use of projectiles to spread the gas. Because they proposed to release gas from cylinders on the ground, they claimed that they had not broken the convention.

The Germans first used chlorine gas in January 1915 at Lódz in Poland, to little effect. However, on April 22, 1915, weather conditions at Ypres in Belgium were just right. Chlorine gas was released from 5,700 cylinders over a 3.5-mile (5.6-km) front. The Allies suffered 15,000 casualties, with 5,000 deaths, enabling the Germans to advance more than a mile (1.6 km) through the Allies' lines without firing a shot. But this use of chlorine had been only an experiment, so the German command had not assembled enough troops to take advantage of the 4-mile (6.4-km) gap that opened before them.

The Allied Response

The Allies responded quickly to these chemical attacks. Soon they were issuing their troops with gas masks, and using chlorine gas themselves. The Germans next introduced phosgene, a gas that first caused irritation to the throat and eyes, and then choked its victims by filling their lungs with

By 1909 Haber had established that he could produce large quantities of ammonia with an iron catalyst at a temperature of 932°F (500°C) and a pressure of about 200 atmospheres. Commercial production of ammonia by the "Haber process" began in 1913, the year before World War I started. By 1918, thanks to Haber, Germany had remained virtually self-sufficient in its supply of this vital chemical throughout the years of fighting.

fluid. Death could take a torturous 48 hours. The Germans also began using bombs and artillery shells to target gas attacks. Once more the Allies did the same.

In 1917, the Germans added mustard gas to their arsenal of chemical weaponry; this caused terrible blistering. By 1918 both sides were using mustard gas in large quantities. In fact, gas attacks—feared by all, terrible to experience, and producing agonizing deaths—had little impact on the course of the war. Of an overall total of 6.9 million deaths, only about 91,000 were

A painting by American artist John Singer Sargent (1856-1925) captures the horror of chemical warfare. A line of men, blinded by gas, cling to their companions as they stumble through a corpse-strewn battlefield.

caused by gas. Some German scientists refused to participate in the chemical warfare program, but Haber seems to have felt little guilt over his work in this field. "A man belongs to the world in times of peace but to his country in times of war," he insisted.

AN UNTIMELY AWARD

In 1911 Haber became director of the Kaiser Wilhelm Institute for Physical Chemistry in Berlin, and on the outbreak of World War I in August 1914 Haber put his laboratory at the disposal of the German government. He became a key figure in the development of poison gas as a weapon on the battlefield (see box above).

In 1918 Haber was awarded the Nobel Prize for chemistry "for the synthesis of ammonia from its elements, nitrogen and hydrogen." The process that Haber invented had produced weapons responsible for the death and disablement of millions of people in the war, so it seemed to many that this was an odd award to make at this time. Many French and British scientists felt that Haber's role in developing German chemical warfare made him unfit to receive such an award and that he had "initiated a mode of warfare which is to the everlasting discredit of Germany."

EXTRACTING GOLD FROM THE SEA

Ever the patriot, Haber sought another way to serve his country. At the end of World War I the Allies ordered Germany to pay a very large fine as a punishment. Some of this was to be paid in gold. The Allies hoped that the burden of such costs would halt any military aggression by Germany. Haber knew that the world's oceans contained billions of tons of gold, and he began to try to recover this gold from seawater and so help free Germany from her huge debts. In 1923 he set up a laboratory on the liner *Hansa* and began trying to extract gold from the Atlantic Ocean, but the project was unsuccessful and was abandoned in 1927.

A VICTIM OF THE NAZI PURGE

After the war Haber's institute in Berlin became the world's leading center of research in physical chemistry. Haber had close links with industry, and he began building better relations with foreign scientists. In 1930 he founded the Japan Institute, which had bases in Berlin and Tokyo, to forge closer cultural and scientific links between the two countries.

In January 1933, Adolf Hitler (1889–1945) became Chancellor of Germany. The Nazi party he headed blamed the Jews for the country's economic and social problems and passed a series of anti-Jewish laws. In April 1933 a new Civil Service Law prevented the employment of anyone not of pure German descent. All university teachers and professors in Germany were employed by the state, and very large numbers of them, particularly scientists and doctors, were Jewish. Hitler stated that if the loss of Jewish scientists meant the "annihilation of German science, then we shall do without science for a few years."

For Jewish scientists, however distinguished or old, leaving the country was the only sensible course of action, even though the costs of doing so were high. It meant abandoning one's family home, all financial assets, and perhaps a laboratory or a professional position built up over a lifetime. Non-Jewish German scientists looked on hopelessly as they saw the might of German science dwindle away before their eyes. Nobel prize-winners, major mathematicians, physicists, and chemists were all forced to flee their own country.

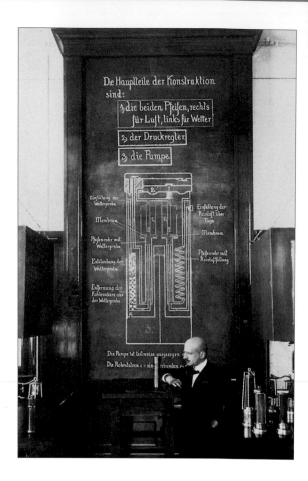

Haber in his laboratory in 1913. His past loyalty did not count for anything under Hitler's regime. In 1933 "the Jew Haber" resigned his position and left Germany for ever.

Haber was Jewish. At first his leading position, famous patriotism, and previous service to the state gave him some protection. Those, like Haber, who had fought in the 1914–18 war were exempt from the Civil Service Law. Unofficially, Haber was told that—as long as he made no fuss—his position would be secure. Haber would have none of this, though, and he resigned his post. There was no turning back. Haber left Germany for the final time in the summer of 1933. He had already been invited to work in Cambridge, England, by Sir William Pope (1870–1939), the chemist who had been in charge of Britain's own chemical warfare program. But Haber worked in Cambridge for only a brief period. Soon after his move to England, while on vacation in Switzerland on January 29, 1934, he died of a heart attack.

Before 1880

French chemist Claude-Louis Berthollet (1748–1822) shows that ammonia is a compound of nitrogen and hydrogen

German chemist August Wilhelm von Hofmann (1818–1892) produces synthetic dyes known as magenta, or fuchsine, and "Hofmann's violets"

1893 Haber begins studies on decomposition of organic compounds at high temperatures

1896 Haber publishes *Experimental Studies on Decomposition of Hydrocarbons*

1905 German chemist Johann von Baeyer (1835–1917) wins the Nobel Prize for chemistry for synthesizing indigo

1906 English chemist William Henry Perkin (1838–1907) is honored at a celebration dinner at the Royal Institution in London; it is the 50th anniversary of his discovery of the synthetic dye, mauve

1909 The first 3.5 ounces (100 g) of synthetic ammonia are produced by the Haber process

1912 German industrial chemist Friedrich Karl Rudolf Bergius (1884–1949) uses high pressure, high temperatures, and a catalyst to produce paraffins (alkanes) such as petrol and kerosene from coal dust

1913 The Haber process is developed for commercial production of nitrogen by German chemist Karl Bosch (1874–1940) of Badische Anilin- & Soda-Fabrik in Oppau, Germany

c. 1925 Commercial production of paraffins from coal dust using Bergius's process begins; it will provide important alternative fuel for Germany during World War II (1939–45)

After 1930

1939 Swiss chemist Paul Müller (1899–1965) synthesizes dichlorodiphenyl-trichloroethane (DDT) as an insecticide

1962 *Silent Spring*, by American naturalist Rachel Carson (1907–1964) highlights the devastating effect of modern synthetic chemical pesticides such as DDT on the food chain

---

1880   **1900**   **1910**   **1920**

1888 Wilhelm II (1859–1941) is crowned third German emperor and ninth king of Prussia

1889 At the Hague conference, Germany and 23 other countries agree not to use chemical weapons, "projectiles whose sole object is the diffusion of asphyxiating gases"

1900 The Republican president of the United States, William McKinley (1843–1901), wins re-election on the promise of "four more years of the full dinner pail"

1905 Russian troops in St. Petersburg open fire on workers demonstrating in front of the Winter Palace of Tsar Nicholas II (1868–1918); more than 200 people are killed

1909 The National Negro Committee (later the National Association for the Advancement of Colored People [NAACP]) is founded in the United States

1915 In April at Ypres in Belgium, German soldiers attack French and Canadian troops using chlorine gas; more than 5,000 Allied troops die

1916 In France, the Germans and French each lose 400,000 dead or wounded in the Battle of Verdun

1922 The Union of Soviet Socialist Republics (USSR) is officially established

1924 American inventor Clarence Birdseye (1886–1956), who has seen how the people of Labrador keep food fresh by freezing it, sets up the General Seafood Company selling a range of frozen foods

1928 In the Soviet Union Communist leader Josef Stalin (1879–1953) tries to force peasants to work state-owned farms, or "collectives," as part of his first Five-Year Plan; those who resist are killed or sent to labor camps

ALAN TURING

1912-1954

"One day ladies will take their computers for walks in the park and tell each other, 'My little computer said such a funny thing this morning!'"

Alan Turing

A MATHEMATICAL GENIUS, ALAN TURING LED THE WAY FOR THE DEVELOPMENT OF ELECTRONIC COMPUTERS, AND IMAGINED THE POTENTIAL OF ARTIFICIAL INTELLIGENCE—THE ABILITY OF A COMPUTER TO PERFORM TASKS IN THE WAY A HUMAN MIGHT. HE WAS ALSO INSTRUMENTAL IN DEVELOPING THE MACHINE THAT CRACKED THE SECRET "ENIGMA" CODE USED BY THE GERMANS IN WORLD WAR II (1939-45).

Alan Mathison Turing was born in London on June 23, 1912. At age 13 he was sent to Sherborne, a boarding school in southwest England, but he was not particularly happy there. However, Turing was outstanding at mathematics. He sought refuge from loneliness in the science laboratory, often carrying out chemistry experiments in his own time. Turing then befriended a boy called Christopher Morcom, who shared his love of mathematics. Early in 1931 Morcom became sick and died suddenly. Turing was devastated.

In October 1931 Turing went to study mathematics at King's College, part of Cambridge University. He completed his studies in 1934 and was given a graduate research position at his college.

THE SEARCH FOR MATHEMATICAL LOGIC

Early in 1935 Turing attended some lectures by Max Newman (1897-1984), a British mathematician with an interest in mathematical logic—the branch of science concerned with the role of mathematics in formal analysis. Mathematicians were much concerned at the beginning of the 20th century with the question of whether all mathematical truths could be derived from purely logical foundations. A key figure in the field was British philosopher Bertrand Russell (1872-1970). With English mathematician Alfred North Whitehead (1861-1947), Russell wrote *Principia Mathematica* (1910-13). Whitehead and Russell believed that in their book they had a complete, logical system within which all valid mathematical formulas could be proved.

Newman's lectures covered this work, as well as that of the Austrian-born American philosopher and mathematician Kurt Gödel (1906-1978), who had

Turing running at King's College, Cambridge. A good athlete, he often ran distances of about 30 miles (48 km).

challenged Russell and Whitehead's argument. Gödel had actually been trying to prove the same point as them; however, he believed there must be true statements about numbers that cannot be proved in their system, and which were therefore "undecidable."

Newman's lectures also discussed the work of the German mathematician David Hilbert (1862–1943). In 1900 Hilbert had posed some 23 problems that he thought needed to be solved in order to advance the study of mathematics, some of which are still unsolved today. Hilbert thought that a set of instructions, or "algorithms," might be found to work out if a statement were undecidable. If so, mathematicians could remove the undecidable statements from their calculations.

KEY DATES

1935	Becomes interested in mathematical logic while doing mathematical research at Cambridge
1936–38	Continues to work on problems of mathematical logic at Princeton University, New Jersey, U.S.
1937	His key work, *On Computable Numbers, with an Application to the Decision Problem*, is published
1939	Is posted to the top-secret Government Code and Cypher School, Bletchley Park, Buckinghamshire, England
1942	Helps build the digital computing machine, Colossus
1945	Works on the ACE computer at the British National Physical Laboratory
1948	Works on the Mark I computer at Manchester University

ALAN TURING

THE DREAM MACHINE

Turing began to study mathematical logic more deeply. He devised an imaginary "machine" to prove that a number of important mathematical problems could have no effective decision process. Turing thought of his machine as being made up of an infinitely long tape, divided into an infinite number of cells containing instructions, and a device that read these instructions. The machine would be able to calculate anything for which there was an algorithm. If the algorithm told it how to determine whether or not a number was prime, the machine would be able to do so; if the algorithm told the machine the rules of chess, the machine could play chess. There could be any number of these machines doing different tasks.

Turing then imagined a single machine that could interpret the instructions for all the individual tasks and so do everything the individual Turing machines could do. He named this a Universal Turing Machine (UTM). Turing had just laid out the principles for a digital computer. The Turing machines can be seen as computer programs, and the UTM as the computer itself. Using his imaginary machine, Turing showed that there will always be undecidable problems in math. While studying at Princeton University in the United States, Turing met the Hungarian-born mathematician Johann von Neumann (1903–1957). He realized the

Bletchley Park was the top-secret headquarters of the Ultra Project set up in World War II. More than 2,000 coded German signals a day were sometimes intercepted, including orders issued by Adolf Hitler (1889–1945).

THE ENIGMA CODE

Enigma machines for sending coded messages were first built in Germany in the 1920s. They were originally intended for industrial and commercial use, but the German military soon became very interested in the devices and began making their own adaptations to the basic design.

When the Germans wanted to send a secret message, they would set the sending machine to a certain key starting position, and type the uncoded message into the machine. The machine had three rotors that scrambled up the message so that it was transmitted in code. The radio operator at the receiving end would set his Enigma machine to the same key starting position, and type the coded message in. The receiving machine would then unscramble it so that the original message could be read. The Enigma machine could be used on billions of settings and be reset at any time, so the Germans believed that the code could never be broken.

German troops send a coded message on an Enigma machine. The Germans never knew their code had been cracked, so they continued to send messages the Allies could unscramble.

Breaking the Code

Most code-breaking depends on analyzing how frequently certain letters appear. The letter E, for example, occurs often in English, but others, such as Q and Z, are rare. If a codebreaker can work out the most and least frequent letters, this is a good starting point for cracking codes. But the Enigma machine was designed to hide the frequencies of letters. Each time a letter was typed in, the rotor moved, so the next time the same letter

Codebreakers at work at Bletchley Park in 1943 (left). The Enigma machine (below) looked like an old-fashioned typewriter. The Bletchley Park unit had two Enigma machines to work with, obtained by British secret agents.

was typed in it would be encoded by a different letter. For example, the first time the letter E appeared it might be represented by A, the second time by X, and the third time by F, and so on. The code was changed daily, so even if a codebreaker solved one day's messages, this counted for nothing on the following day. The team at Bletchley Park faced a daunting task, but they knew that any system has flaws. Their task was to find them.

The first mistake was in the way the Germans transmitted the key to the code. This was three letters corresponding to the starting position of the rotors. Because they thought that the receiver might not get the message clearly, they sent the three-letter key twice. Suppose the key was CAT, then they would type "CAT CAT," which might be encoded as "XSP WRL." The team therefore knew that out of the first six letters of a transmission, the first and fourth letter, the second and fifth, and the third and sixth resulted from the encoding

of the same letters of original text.

On the Enigma machine a letter could never be represented by itself. Code-breakers used this fact to identify "cribs," pieces of text that they guessed might appear in the message, such as, "Nothing to report." These could occur anywhere, but the fact that no letter could be represented by itself made them easier to spot. Identifying such a phrase gave the codebreakers a key to start the task of decipherment.

The breaking of the Enigma code gave the Allies invaluable information about German war plans. The Japanese also had Enigma machines. Intercepted messages revealing Japanese naval plans helped secure vital U.S naval victories in the Pacific. British war leader Winston Churchill (1874–1965) said that the work at Bletchley Park may have shortened the war by five years.

Turing was part of the team that invented the world's first all-electronic digital computing machine, Colossus (above). It was used to decipher the more complicated Lorenz cypher used by the German navy in early 1942. Bombes (right), seen here in an operating unit room, were machines that decoded German signals sent on Enigma machines.

practical possibilities of Turing's work. Back in England, Turing began building a mechanical device to carry out complex calculations, but World War II started in 1939.

BREAKING THE CODE

Soon after the war against Germany began, the British secret service set up the "Ultra Project" at Bletchley Park in southern England to find a way of decoding coded signals sent by the Germans. British radio-operators intercepted hundreds of German military signals daily. They were sent by code via a device called an Enigma machine (see box page 50). The Germans believed this code could not be broken, but the British knew that if they could decipher the code, they would be able to pass on vital information about such things as troop movements and bombing raids to the military planners.

An assortment of people was assembled at Bletchley Park—experts in languages, chess-players, crossword-puzzle solvers, and others thought to have the kind of brain needed to decipher coded messages. Soon Turing joined their number. One Bletchley Park worker recalls: "There was a great degree of tolerance at Bletchley for eccentricities. At least half of the people were absolutely mad. They were geniuses, no doubt many of them were extremely clever, but my goodness they were strange in ordinary life." Even in this company, Turing's behavior stood out and he managed to upset many fellow workers. His pattern of working was also considered odd: he would stay up for days and nights on end and then fall asleep at his desk.

The Enigma code was so complex that codebreakers needed to know the starting position of each of the three rotors in order to decipher each message (see box page 50). There were billions of possible settings. Turing saw that if solutions were to be found in a reasonable time the process would have to be mechanized. So with some of his colleagues at Bletchley Park, Turing developed the "bombe," a form of computer that enabled many possible solutions to codes to be quickly substituted and checked. The first bombe, ready for use in 1940, was rather slow. This improved by late 1941, by which time there were 15 bombes on site and German ciphers were usually decoded within hours of being intercepted. From early 1942, however, German U-boats (submarines) used the more complicated "Lorenz" cypher, and it was not until March 1943 that the codebreakers found the key to deciphering this.

In 1942 electronic technology helped to speed up decoding, and Turing helped build the first all-electronic digital computing machine, known as Colossus. The computer began operating in late 1943.

INTELLIGENT MACHINES

When the war ended in 1945 Turing took a post at the National Physical Laboratory in London, working on the design of a new computer ACE (Automatic Computing

Alan Turing (seen standing) talks to colleagues working on the Ferranti Mark I computer, completed in 1951.

Engine). In 1946 the first programmable, all-electronic digital computer was completed at the University of Pennsylvania, Philadelphia; meanwhile Turing's project was hampered by a lack of government funding. He eventually decided to return to Cambridge, but in 1948 he was invited by Max Newman to move to Manchester University in northwest England, where Newman was professor of mathematics. There Turing began work on the computer known as the Ferranti Mark I.

Two years later Turing published "Computing Machinery and Intelligence," proposing that it would be possible to make computers appear to be thinking for themselves in ways that humans would. This is known as artificial intelligence. To test this theory Turing devised what he called the Imitation Game—later known as the Turing Test. A questioner is positioned on one side of a screen; on the other side are a computer and a human. If the questioner cannot decide from each subject's answers which is which, then the computer can be said to be "thinking" as successfully as a human.

A TRAGIC END

In the 1950s, the Cold War was at its height. This was a period of extremely tense relations between the United States and its allies and the Soviet Union and its power bloc in Eastern Europe, which was marked by the rapid build-up of nuclear weapons on both sides. Turing went back to carrying out highly secret decoding work on behalf of the British government at this time. He still carried on his university research, and in 1951 was elected a member of the Royal Society in London.

Turing died of cyanide poisoning in 1954. He was said at the time to have accidentally contaminated his hands while conducting a chemical experiment, but it is possible that he committed suicide after being questioned by the police because he was a homosexual (then an illegal activity in Britain).

THE COMPUTER REVOLUTION

In Turing's day computers were enormous machines. It seemed they could only get bigger as they became more powerful. Then came two technological advances: the transistor and the microchip.

Transistors, invented in 1947 at the Bell Telephone Laboratories in the United States, are electronic devices that amplify (enlarge) small electric currents, and can switch currents on and off; they made computers much more compact and powerful.

The microchip was invented in 1959. This tiny chip, measuring about 0.15 square inches (1 sq. cm), was made of silicon, a semiconducting material onto which miniature electric circuits could be etched. The early chips carried about 10 transistor circuits; by 1969, 1,000 transistor circuits could be embedded on one chip. Eventually scientists were able to embed hundreds of thousands of transistor circuits and other minute electronic components onto one microchip. The age of the desktop personal computer was born.

A Worldwide Network

Within organizations, computers and databases were linked in networks that made it possible to transfer information from one to another. Work on developing a system that could transfer information between networks began in the 1960s. The ARPAnet, linking four sites, went live in 1969. By the late 1980s it had grown into the Internet, linking computer networks across the world.

Then British software engineer Tim Berners-Lee (1955–), devised a system to allow people to work together via their computers by delivering documents across the Internet. In 1991 it was launched as the World Wide Web. The system revolutionized the Internet. Within five years, the number of users had risen to 40 million.

The New York Times's front page is displayed online. The introduction of the World Wide Web, allowing users anywhere in the world to research and share information over the Internet, opened up a new era of global communication.

The New York Times on the Web

Back Forward Stop Refresh Home Favorites History Search AutoFill Larger Smaller Print Mail Preferences

Address: http://www.nytimes.com/

     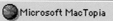 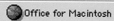

Live Home Page   Apple Computer   Apple Support   Apple Store   Microsoft MacTopia   Office for Macintosh   Internet Explor

The New York Times
ON THE WEB

UPDATED TUESDAY, MAY 22, 2001 8:50 AM ET | Personalize Your Weather

TIFFANY &

CLASSIFIEDS
Automobiles
Job Market
Real Estate
Personals
All Classifieds

NEWS
Quick News
NYT Front Page
Arts
Business
Health
International
National
New York Region
Obituaries
Politics
Science

Search [   ]   Today's News ▲▼ ⊙
Go to Advanced Search

Senate Turns Down Efforts To Change Tax-Cut Measure
By DAVID E. ROSENBAUM
Republicans maintained a united front as the Senate rejected efforts to change the tax-cut bill, President Bush's top legislative priority. A vote on the measure is expected on Tuesday. Go to Article
• Senators Reprise Familiar Refrains on Tax Cut

Firestone to Stop Sales to Ford
By KEITH BRADSHER
Bridgestone, acting ahead of Ford's expected effort to

(AFP)Secretary of State Colin L. Powell appointed a diplomat to shepherd a

INSIDE

SPORTS
Still Tough to Catch
Barry Sanders' retirement in 1999 remains a mystery. Will he come back to football?

MARKETS

Dow Jones Industrials

Before 1930

British philosopher Bertrand Russell (1872–1970), and British mathematician Alfred North Whitehead (1861–1947) publish *Principia Mathematica*

American philosopher Kurt Gödel (1906–1978) demonstrates that there must be statements about numbers that cannot be proved or disproved and so are "undecidable"

1931 Turing studies mathematics at Cambridge University, England

1934 Turing takes a graduate research position at Cambridge

1935 Turing attends lectures given by British mathematician Max Newman (1897–1984) on mathematical logic

1942 Turing helps to build the first all-electronic digital computing machine, called Colossus

1946 The first programmable, all-electronic digital computer, the Electronic Numerical Integrator and Calculator (ENIAC), is completed at the University of Pennsylvania

1947 The transistor is invented at the Bell Telephone Laboratories in the United States

1950 Turing publishes his paper on artificial intelligence, *Computing Machinery and Intelligence*

1951 The Universal Automatic Computer (UNIVAC), installed in the Census Bureau in Philadelphia, is the first to store information on magnetic tape

1956 FORTRAN, the first computer programming language, is developed in the United States

1959 The microchip is invented

1964 The first word-processor is introduced by IBM in the United States and Europe

1969 ARPAnet links four sites, allowing transfer of information between computers and databases

After 1970

1991 The World Wide Web, a system originally devised by British software engineer Tim Berners-Lee (1955–) is launched

---

1930 **1940** **1950** **1960**

1934–1936 Communist leader Mao Zedong (1893–1976) takes his troops on the "Long March" from southeast China to their new headquarters in northwest China, 5,000 miles (8,050 km) away

1936 American novelist Margaret Mitchell (1900–1949) publishes *Gone With the Wind*; the book sells millions of copies and the story becomes an Oscar-winning film in 1959

1941 German leader Adolf Hitler (1889–1945) launches a three-pronged attack on the Soviet Union (Germany's former ally), codenamed Operation Barbarossa

1943 Allied forces land in Italy; Italy surrenders unconditionally and declares war on Germany, its former ally

1949 English writer George Orwell (1903–1950) publishes *Nineteen Eighty-Four*, his grim vision of a future society in which "Big Brother is watching you"

1952 A Republican landslide in the U.S. general election gives Dwight D. Eisenhower (1890–1969) the largest ever share of the popular vote

1955 In Montgomery, Alabama, African-American Rosa Parks (1913–2005) refuses to move to the back of a bus, leading to a local bus boycott by African-Americans demanding civil rights

1957 A treaty signed in Rome by Belgium, France, the German Federal Republic, Italy, Luxembourg, and the Netherlands, establishes the European Economic Community (EEC)

1961 *Catch 22*, which paints a blackly comic picture of the experience of serving in the U.S. Army Airforce in World War II (1939–45), eventually becomes a massive bestseller for its author, the American Joseph Heller (1923–1999)

JONAS SALK

1914–1995

"You never have an idea of what you might accomplish. All that you do is pursue a question and see where it leads."

Jonas Salk

IN 1955 THE AMERICAN MICROBIOLOGIST JONAS SALK DEVELOPED THE FIRST EFFECTIVE VACCINE AGAINST THE ACUTE INFECTIOUS VIRAL DISEASE KNOWN AS POLIOMYELITIS, OR POLIO. THIS DISEASE CAN AFFECT THE SPINAL CORD AND BRAIN AND CAUSE PARALYSIS. SALK WENT ON TO SEARCH FOR A VACCINE AGAINST ACQUIRED IMMUNE DEFICIENCY SYNDROME (AIDS).

Jonas Salk was born in New York City on October 28, 1914, to Polish-Jewish immigrant parents. Jonas graduated in surgery in 1934 and entered the New York University College of Medicine. There he worked with the microbiologist Thomas Francis, Jr. 1900–1969), carrying out research into the epidemiology of influenza (epidemiology is the science concerned with the pattern and control of disease in a population). By 1940 Francis had isolated two distinct types of influenza virus.

Salk then worked at the Mount Sinai Hospital in New York City, but in 1942 he joined the Virus Research Unit that Francis now headed at the University of Michigan School of Public Health. The unit had been set up by the US Army to develop a vaccine against influenza. A vaccine gives immunity against a particular disease by stimulating the production of antibodies to destroy the invading microorganisms that cause it. Francis developed "killed-virus" vaccines against both types of influenza virus. With this type of vaccine, the virus has been made inactive without completely destroying it. Vaccines are also given in "attenuated" form, when the virus or other microorganism is still alive, but its ability to cause infection has been reduced.

In 1947 Salk moved to the University of Pittsburgh, Pennsylvania, where he took charge of a team that was conducting a program to investigate viral diseases. It was there, working in collaboration with the National Foundation for Infantile Paralysis, that Salk began working to develop a polio vaccine that would give people immunity against the disease.

AN ANCIENT DISEASE

Polio is an acute infectious disease: symptoms include fever, sore throat, and vomiting. In most cases the patient makes a full recovery after an attack. However,

KEY DATES

1934 Graduates in surgery from the City College of New York

1938 Works with microbiologist Thomas Francis, Jr., seeking an influenza vaccine

1939 Graduates in medicine from New York University College of Medicine

1940–42 Works at Mount Sinai Hospital, New York City

1942–44 Works on influenza vaccines at the Virus Research Unit of the University of Michigan School of Public Health

1947 Heads the virus research laboratory at the University of Pittsburgh, Pennsylvania; begins work on polio vaccine

1954 Clinical trials of the vaccine begin

1955 Salk's polio vaccine declared safe and effective on April 12

1963 Opens the Salk Institute for Biological Studies in La Jolla

1972 Publishes *Man Unfolding*

1981 Publishes *World Population and Human Values: A New Reality*

Jonas Salk studies some of the racks of vials containing his polio vaccine. Initial trials suggested that the vaccine was highly effective in preventing polio; large-scale clinical trials began in 1954.

JONAS SALK

about 20 percent of patients can suffer permanent paralysis and muscle loss. If the upper part of the spinal cord is infected, chest muscles may become paralyzed, affecting breathing. If the brain stem is affected the patient loses the use of the muscles involved in swallowing and talking and can choke to death. It is not difficult to see why polio was greatly feared.

Polio is believed to have occurred throughout human history. A figure carved on a pillar in ancient Egypt between 1580 BC and 1350 BC may depict a polio victim. One of the most famous victims of polio was Franklin D. Roosevelt (1882–1945), four-times president of the United States, who was stricken by the disease in 1921. In the mid-20th century, polio had reached epidemic levels in the United States. The disease was passed on at school or at crowded swimming pools and other places where young people

A high-powered photograph of the virus particles—known as virions—responsible for poliomyelitis. Virions have a simple structure and are less than 30 nanometers (30 billionths of a meter) across. A method of growing viruses on embryo tissue was developed, and this paved the way for the testing of Salk's polio vaccine.

met, and thousands of new cases were reported each year. Many died; others were left paralyzed, with wasted limbs. Most unfortunate were those whose respiratory muscles were affected. Although the "iron lung," developed in 1932, kept them alive by forcing air in and out of their lungs, they had to spend their lives flat on their backs in bed. Massive efforts were directed toward finding a cure for the disease. The National Foundation for Infantile Paralysis, which supported Salk's research, was at the head of a huge publicity campaign to fight polio.

A polio victim looks at a comic book in his "iron lung" (right); the lung breathes for the patient, whose respiratory muscles have been paralyzed. Another young victim, pictured in 1955 (below), adjusts to life in a wheelchair.

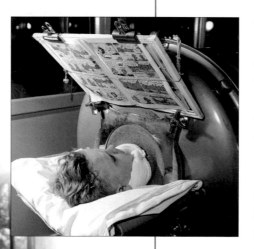

THE SEARCH FOR A VACCINE

Polio is caused by a virus—a tiny micro-organism too small to be seen with any except the most powerful scanning electron microscope. Viruses cannot be grown in a test tube; they can reproduce only inside living cells. In 1948 American microbiologist John Enders (1897–1985) and virologists Frederick Robbins (1916–2003) and Thomas Weller (1915–2008) found a way of growing viruses in tissue taken from chick embryos, using the antibiotic penicillin to keep the material free from bacterial infection.

This gave Salk the breakthrough he needed. He obtained viruses from the spinal cords of polio victims and grew them in the new medium. Detailed tests revealed that there are three distinct types of poliovirus. By 1952 Salk had produced a killed-virus vaccine effective against all three.

After testing the vaccine successfully in monkeys, he administered it to children who had recovered from the disease. Because they had acquired immunity, they could not catch it again, but after receiving the vaccine,

the quantity of virus-fighting antibodies in their blood increased. Then Salk tried it on himself, his wife, and three sons, as well as other volunteers. Everyone injected with the vaccine produced antibodies against the three poliovirus types, and no one became sick.

The next step was to test the vaccine in a large clinical trial. This would require larger amounts of vaccine than Salk's laboratory could produce, so five drug companies were licenced to produce it. Sadly, there were faults in some of the vaccine used. As a result 204 people contracted polio and 11 died. Salk insisted that all further vaccines be tested by the public health service, and no more accidents occurred.

In the clinical trials that began in 1954, 1.8 million American schoolchildren received either the vaccine or a placebo (a harmless substance). Results showed that the vaccine was safe and effective, and on April 12, 1955 a vast public inoculation campaign began. In 1952 there had been 58,000 new cases of polio

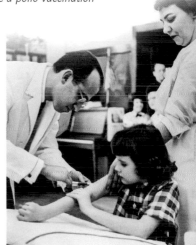

Children line up to receive a polio vaccination at an emergency center in Chicago in 1956 (above), and Jonas Salk administers the injection to a Pittsburgh schoolchild (right). Between 1956 and 1958, 200 million injections were given in the United States, virtually eliminating the disease there.

in the United States; by 1962 the number had fallen to around only 1,000—a remarkable success.

Killed-virus vaccines like Salk's polio vaccine have a drawback over live-attenuated vaccines: they have to be administered in greater quantities and over a longer period. People had to receive two or three injections of Salk's vaccine several weeks apart, followed by booster doses 6 to 12 months later and in subsequent years. At the time that Salk was testing his vaccine, Albert Sabin (1906–1993) was completing his work on a live attenuated vaccine, which could be given once only in oral form (by mouth), often on a sugar lump (see box below). Its attractions were obvious, and once it had passed its clinical trials, it replaced the Salk vaccine.

RECOGNITION AND HONOR

Salk's conquest of the polio threat in the United States made him a national hero, a little to the annoyance of colleagues who felt their own contributions to the development of the vaccine were overlooked. Salk also won international recognition, and in 1955 he was made a member of the French Legion of Honor.

In 1957 Salk was appointed professor of experimental medicine at Pittsburgh University, Pennsylvania. In 1963 he become director of the Institute for Biological Studies in San Diego, California. With the financial backing of the National Foundation for Infantile Paralysis he established the Salk Institute for Biological Studies in La Jolla. He later tried to develop vaccines against multiple sclerosis, a chronic disease of the central nervous system, and AIDS (Acquired Immune Deficiency Syndrome), a virally induced condition that destroys the ability to fight disease. Salk was awarded the Presidential Medal of Freedom in 1977, and died on June 23, 1995.

THE SUGAR LUMP VACCINE

Albert Sabin encourages a reluctant five-year-old Brazilian boy to swallow a sugar lump laced with his polio vaccine.

Albert Sabin first became interested in polio in the 1930s. In 1936 he and his colleagues were the first to succeed in growing the polio virus, which they obtained from monkeys, in human nervous tissue outside the body. Unlike Salk, Sabin believed that exposure to a living virus was the only way to guarantee lifetime immunity to polio, and he spent many years developing a weakened (attenuated) form of the virus by growing it in monkey kidney tissue. By 1957 he had isolated strains of each of the three types of polio virus that were not strong enough to produce the disease itself but were capable of stimulating the production of antibodies.

Large-scale trials of Salk's vaccine had only just been completed in the United States, and rather than launch another trial on the American public, Sabin obtained permission from the Soviet authorities to test his vaccine in Russia—a bold move at a time when the Cold War between America and the Communist bloc was at its height. The vaccine was also licenced for testing in eastern Europe and Britain, and from 1961 it was available for use in the United States. The Sabin vaccine is often given to children on a sugar lump. When administered by mouth it causes an infection in a person's intestines. This triggers the forming of the antibodies to resist the polio virus, without making the person sick. Like Salk, Sabin did not take out a patent on his vaccine, insisting that it be delivered free of charge. During the early 1960s about 100 million European children and a similar number of Americans of all ages received the vaccine.

Before 1940

English physician Edward Jenner (1749–1823) carries out the first vaccination

American army surgeon Walter Reed (1851–1902) discovers the yellow fever virus, the first human virus to be identified

American scientist Thomas Milton Rivers (1888–1962) distinguishes between bacteria and viruses

1942 The first influenza vaccine is introduced

1947 Salk begins work on polio vaccine

1948 American microbiologist John Enders (1897–1985), and virologists Frederick Robbins (1916–2003) and Thomas Weller (1915–2008) grow poliovirus

1952 Salk's polio vaccine is ready for testing

1954 Clinical trials of the polio vaccine begin

1955 Salk's polio vaccine is declared safe and effective on April 12

1956 Scottish virologist Alick Isaacs (1921–1967) discovers interferon, an antibody produced by cells infected by viruses

1957 Russian-born American biologist Albert Sabin (1906–1993) develops an oral vaccine for polio that is delivered on a sugar lump

1961 Sabin's oral vaccine for polio becomes available

1963 The Salk Institute for Biological Studies opens in La Jolla, California

1967 The global smallpox eradication program, conducted by the World Health Organization (WHO), begins

1971 Sabin is presented with the U.S. National Medal of Science

1977 Salk is awarded the Presidential Medal of Freedom

1980 WHO declares that smallpox has been eradicated throughout the world

After 1980

1988 WHO begins a campaign to eradicate polio by the year 2000. The target is later revised to 2005

2005 The annual number of polio cases worldwide falls to 1,940, a massive reduction on the 1988 figure of 350,000 cases

---

1940 | **1950** | **1960** | **1970**

1941 Nylon, first produced by the Dupont plant in the United States, is increasingly being used to meet the demand for parachutes for the armed services fighting in World War II (1939–45)

1945 Harry S. Truman (1884–1972) becomes 33rd president of the United States after the death of Franklin D. Roosevelt (1882–1945)

1951 The 22nd Amendment of the U.S. Constitution is ratified, providing for a maximum U.S. presidential term of eight years

1953 The American tennis star Maureen "Little Mo" Connolly (1934–1969) is the first woman to win the "Grand Slam" of all four major tennis titles (American, Australian, British, and French) in one year

1959 The Guggenheim Museum is completed in New York. It is the last major work by American architect Frank Lloyd Wright (1867–1959)

1965 The British rock group the Rolling Stones release "(I Can't Get No) Satisfaction," which will become one of their greatest hits

1966 Indira Gandhi (1917–1984), daughter of the former prime minister Jawaharlal Nehru (1889–1964), becomes India's first female prime minister

1972 *The Godfather*, the saga of an Italian-American Mafia family, starring Marlon Brando (1924–2004) and Al Pacino (1939–), is a cinema box-office hit

1977 In South Africa Steve Biko (1946–1977), the leader of the "black consciousness" campaign, dies in police custody

1979 In Tehran, Iran, students angry that their overthrown leader, the shah, is receiving medical treatment in the United States, seize the U.S. embassy and take 66 hostages; the hostages are finally released in 1981

GLOSSARY

Amino acids An important class of organic (carbon-containing) compounds.

Anatomy The structure and form of biological organisms.

Antibiotics Substances that kill or prevent the growth of other microorganisms. They include penicillins; they are used in the treatment of infection by bacteria or fungi.

Antibodies and antigens Antibodies are defense proteins made by some white cells in the body to counter invading proteins known as antigens. Antibodies bind to antigens, tagging them for destruction by phagocytes (white blood cells that destroy invading bodies), or by activating a chemical system that makes the antigen harmless.

Archeology The study of the past through identification and interpretation of the material remains of human cultures.

Astrology The study of the motions and positions of the planets, Sun, and Moon, in order to predict their imagined influence on the future by the means of astrological charts or horoscopes. No such influence exists, and astrology is not a science.

Astronomy The study of the origin, motion, and composition of material in the universe.

Atmosphere The gaseous envelope around the Earth or any other celestial body. The atmosphere around Earth contains enough oxygen to support animal and plant life.

Bacteria Single-celled microorganisms. Some exist harmlessly alongside host cells; others live in cells or body cavities and produce toxins that damage the host.

Bacteriology The science that deals with bacteria, their characteristics, and activities.

Bacteriophage A virus that attacks bacteria.

Cathode A negatively charged electrode.

Cathode ray A stream of electrons emitted by a cathode when heated.

Cathode-ray tube A vacuum tube containing a heated cathode and an anode, in which a beam of electrons is focused onto a fluorescent screen to give a visible spot of light. The device is used, for example, in television sets.

Celestial body Any of the bodies in the universe, such as planets, stars, and comets.

Chemistry The science concerned with elements and compounds, with the atoms and molecules that make them up, and with the chemical reactions between them.

Comet A celestial body that travels around the Sun, usually in a large elliptical orbit.

Electric charge A property of matter that exists in two forms: positive and negative.

Electric current A flow of electric charge through a conductor.

Electricity The effect of charged particles at rest and in motion. Electricity is used to provide a very adaptable form of energy.

Energy The capacity for doing work. Types of energy include light, sound, and nuclear energy. Energy can be converted from one form to another, but the total amount of mass-energy in the universe stays the same.

Force In mechanics, the influence that changes a body from a state of rest to one of motion; or changes its rate of motion; or distorts it.

Galaxy Any of the star systems containing stars, gases, dust, and planets.

Germ A common term for a microorganism capable of causing disease. The "germ theory," developed by Louis Pasteur correctly identified microorganisms rather than miasma as the cause of infections.

Gravity The force of attraction between all matter. It plays a vital role in the behavior of the universe: the gravitational attraction of the Sun is what keeps the planets in their orbits, for example. The theory that gravitational force existed throughout the universe was first advanced by the English scientist Isaac Newton.

Immunity The ability to resist infection by viruses, bacteria, and other disease-causing microorganisms.

Immunization The process of conferring immunity, particularly by inoculation.

Inoculation The injection or introduction of microorganisms or their products into living tissues in order to produce immunity.

Mathematics The key tool of all science, concerned with the study of number, shape, quantity, space, and their interrelationships.

Mechanics The branch of mathematics dealing with the actions of forces on objects.

Motion Movement; the process of change in the position of one object relative to another.

Nitrogen A gaseous element that forms almost 80 percent of the Earth's atmosphere by volume. It is a constituent of all plant and animal tissues (in proteins and nucleic acids). Nitrogen compounds are used to make foods, drugs, fertilizers, dyes, and explosives. It is used in the Haber process to make ammonia.

Nobel prize A prize established in 1901 with a bequest from the Swedish chemist Alfred Nobel, the inventor of dynamite. The prize may be awarded annually for outstanding contributions to chemistry, physics, physiology or medicine, literature, economics (added in 1968), and peace.

Orbit The path of a celestial body revolving under the influence of gravity; also the path of an electron around the atomic nucleus.

Organic chemistry The branch of chemistry that deals with carbon compounds. Organic compounds form the basic stuff of living tissue.

Organism Any living animal or plant, including any bacterium or virus.

Pathology The branch of medicine that deals with the cause, origin, nature, and effect of disease.

Planet In the solar system, any of the nine celestial bodies revolving around the Sun in an elliptical orbit and illuminated by light from the Sun. There are also planets orbiting other stars.

Radio waves Electromagnetic radiations with very long wavelengths and low energy.

Star A large incandescent gaseous ball held together by its own gravity. The Sun is a star.

Universe The collection of all existing matter, energy, and space.

Vaccination Method of giving immunity against infectious disease caused by bacteria or viruses.

Virology The branch of medicine concerned with the study of viruses and the diseases they cause.

Viruses Tiny parasitic organisms that can reproduce only inside the cell of their host. Viruses replicate by invading host cells and taking over the cell's machinery for DNA replication and protein synthesis.

FURTHER RESOURCES

PUBLICATIONS

ASTRONOMY AND COSMOLOGY
Cornell, James. *The First Stargazers: An Introduction to the Origins of Astronomy.* New York: Scribner, 1981.

BIOCHEMISTRY
Needham, Joseph. *The Chemistry of Life: Eight Lectures on the History of Biochemistry.* New York: Cambridge University Press, 2008.

Stoker, H. Stephen, and Michael R. Slabaugh. *General, Organic, and Biochemistry.* Glenview, IL: Scott, Foresman, 1981.

COMPUTING
Collier, Bruce, and James MacLachlan. *Charles Babbage and the Engines of Perfection.* New York: Oxford University Press, 1998.

Dunn, John M. *The Computer Revolution.* San Diego, CA: Lucent, 2002.

Gottfried, Ted. *Alan Turing: The Architect of the Computer Age.* New York: Franklin Watts, 1996.

O'Regan, Gerard. *A Brief History of Computing.* New York: Springer, 2008.

Schneiderman, Ron. *Computers: From Babbage to the Fifth Generation.* New York: Franklin Watts, 1986.

Spencer, Donald D. *Great Men and Women of Computing.* 2nd ed. Ormond Beach, FL: Camelot, 1999.

Spencer, Donald D. *The Timetable of Computers: A Chronology of the Most Important People and Events in the History of Computers.* Ormond Beach, FL: Camelot, 1999.

Wade, Mary Dodson. *Ada Byron Lovelace: The Lady and the Computer.* New York: Dillon, 1994.

EARLY SCIENCE
Adler, Mortimer J. *Aristotle for Everybody: Difficult Thought Made Easy.* New York: Touchstone, 1997.

Barnes, Jonathan. *Aristotle: A Very Short Introduction.* New York: Oxford University Press, 2001.

Landels, John G. *Engineering in the Ancient World.* Berkeley, CA: University of California Press, 2000.

Lennox, James G. *Aristotle's Philosophy of Biology: Studies in the Origins of Life Science.* New York: Cambridge University Press, 2001.

Spangenburg, Ray, and Diane K. Moser. *The History of Science from the Ancient Greeks to the Scientific Revolution.* New York: Facts on File, 2004.

Strathern, Paul. *Aristotle in 90 Minutes.* Chicago: I.R. Dee, 1996.

MATHEMATICS
Burton, David M. *The History of Mathematics: An Introduction.* 6th ed. Boston: WCB McGraw-Hill, 2005.

Haven, Kendall F. *Marvels of Math: Fascinating Reads and Awesome Activities.* Englewood, CO: Teacher Ideas Press, 1998.

Johnson, Art. *Famous Problems and Their Mathematicians.* Englewood, CO: Teacher Ideas Press, 1999.

Katz, Victor J. *A History of Mathematics: An Introduction.* Reading, MA: Addison-Wesley, 1998.

McLeish, John. *The Story of Numbers.* New York: Fawcett Columbine, 1994.

Phillips, George M. *Two Millennia of Mathematics: From Archimedes to Gauss.* New York: Springer, 2000.

Stillwell, John. *Mathematics and Its History.* New York: Springer, 2004.

MEDICINE
Bredeson, Carmen. *Jonas Salk: Discoverer of the Polio Vaccine.* Hillside, NJ: Enslow, 1993.

Duin, Nancy, and Jenny Sutcliffe. *A History of Medicine: From Pre-history to the Year 2000.* New York: Simon & Schuster, 1992.

Harding, Anne S. *Milestones in Health and Medicine.* Phoenix, AZ: Oryx, 2000.

Kluger, Jeffrey. *Splendid Solution: Jonas Salk and the Conquest of Polio.* New York: Berkley Books, 2006.

Loudon, Irvine, ed. *Western Medicine: An Illustrated History.* New York: Oxford University Press, 1997.

Nuland, Sherwin B. *Doctors: The Illustrated History of Medical Pioneers.* New York: Black Dog & Leventhaul, 2008.

Royston, Angela. *100 Greatest Medical Discoveries.* Danbury, CT: Grolier Educational, 1997.

TECHNOLOGY
Adair, Gene. *Thomas Alva Edison: Inventing the Electric Age.* New York: Oxford University Press, 1997.

Bruno, Leonard C. *Science and Technology Breakthroughs: From the Wheel to the World Wide Web.* 2 vol. Detroit, MI.: U.X.L., 1998.

Burke, James. *Circles: 50 Round Trips Through History, Technology, Science, Culture.* New York: Simon & Schuster, 2000.

Laidler, Keith J. *To Light Such a Candle: Chapters in the History of Science and Technology.* New York: Oxford University Press, 1998.

McPherson, Stephanie S.. *Alexander Graham Bell.* Mineapolis, MN: Learner, 2007.

Pasachoff, Naomi. *Alexander Graham Bell: Making Connections.* New York: Oxford University Press, 1996.

Williams, Trevor I. *A History of Invention: From Stone Axes to Silicon Chips.* London: Little, Brown, 2004.

WEBSITES

GENERAL SCIENCE
Kapili.com
www.kapili.com/topiclist.html
"Tours" through basic terms and topics of the various subfields in astronomy, biology, chemistry, physics, and geography.

The Sciences Explorer
http://www.thinkquest.org/library/cat_show.html?cat_id=13
Explores the fields of astronomy, biology, chemistry, and physics.

CHEMISTRY
A Brief History of Chemistry
http://library.thinkquest.org/2690/hist/history.html
History of chemistry from black magic to the modern science. Includes a list of Nobel Prize winners for chemistry.

COMPUTING
The History of Computing
http://ei.cs.vt.edu/~history
Collection of links related to the history of computing compiled by J. A. N. Lee at Virginia Tech. Includes links to histories of computing and information on computer companies, programming, machines and calculators, women in computing, and other resources.

MATHEMATICS
The MacTutor History of Mathematics Archive
www-groups.dcs.st-andrews.ac.uk/~history
Very extensive collection of brief biographies of notable mathematicians and brief articles about the history of mathematics.

MEDICINE
Medicine Through Time
http://www.bbc.co.uk/schools/gcsebitesize/history/shp/
Concise descriptions of various phases of medical technology through the ages and around the world, including topics in disease treatment, surgery, hospitals, and public health for each era.

Bold page numbers indicate a major article about the subject.

A

Aerial Experiment Association 38
algorithms 49
ammonia synthesis 44
Analytical Engine 20–22
Analytical Society 18
Appleton, Edward 33
Aristarchus of Samos 7
Aristotle **4–9**
Arkwright, Richard 17
Aristotelian logic 8
ARPAnet 54
Automatic Computing Engine 53

B

Babbage, Charles **18–23**
Baeyer, Johann von 43, 47
Bardeen, John 40
Batchelor, Charles 28
Bell, Alexander Graham 27, 33, **34–41**
Bell, Melvin 34, 35
Bell Telephone Company 38–39
Benz, Karl Friedrich 27
Bergius, Friedrich Karl Rudolf 47
Berliner, Emile 32
Berners-Lee, Tim 54
Berthollet, Claude-Louis 47
Blériot, Louis 41
Bletchley Park 51, 52–53
Bolívar, Simón 15
Bosch, Karl 47
Boulton, Matthew 13, 14
Brattain, Walter 40
Brindley, James 17
Byron, Lord 21, 22

C

calculus 18
Carson, Rachel 47
Cartwright, Edmund 17
Catch-me-who-can 15
Chappe, Claude 25, 26, 33
chemical warfare 44–45
Churchill, Winston 51

Cinématographe 30
codebreakers 50–54
Cooke, William 25
Copernicus, Nicolaus 9
Ctesias 6

D

Darwin, Charles 6
Davy, Humphry 28
Democritus 9
difference engine 20–21
Dixon, William 30
duplex 27
dyes, artificial 43

E

Earthly elements 8
Eastman, George 30, 33
Edison, Thomas Alva **24–33**
Electric Light Company 28
electricity generation 30
Enders, John 58, 61
Enigma machine 50–51
Eudoxus of Cnidus 9
Evans, Oliver 16

F

Faraday, Michael 24, 36, 41
Firestone, Harvey 32
Ford, Henry 32, 33
Francis, Thomas, Jr. 56
Franklin, Benjamin 17
Fulton, Robert 17

G

Galilei, Galileo 7, 9
Gauss, Karl 23
Gödel, Kurt 48, 55
gold extraction 46
Gould, Jay 27
Grand Trunk Herald 24
Guericke, Otto von 13

H

Haber, Fritz **42–47**
Haber process 44
Hargreaves, James 17
Herschel, John 18
Hilbert, David 49
History of Animals 6
Hitler, Adolf 46, 50
Hofmann, August Wilhelm von 47

horsepower 16
Hubbard, Gardiner Greene 36, 38
hydrofoil 40

I

influenza vaccination 56
iron lung 58
Isaacs, Alick 61

J

Jenner, Edward 61

K

Keller, Helen 40
kinetograph 30
kinetoscope 30
Kruesi, John 28

L

Langley, Samuel 41
Leibniz, Gottfried 18, 23
Liebig, Justus von 42
light bulb, electric 28–30
logarithms 18
Lovelace, Ada **18–23**
Lumière, Auguste 30, 33
Lumière, Louis 30, 33

M

Marconi, Guglielmo 33, 41
Marey, Étienne-Jules 30
Menabrea, Luigi 22
microchip 54
Milbanke, Annabella 21, 22
Morgan, Augustus de 22
Morse Code 26
Morse, Samuel 26, 33, 41
Müller, Paul 47
Muybridge, Eadweard 30

N

Napier, John 18, 20, 23
Napier's bones 20
Nernst, Walther 44
Neumann, Johann von 50
Newcomen
  engine 10–12
  Thomas 17
Newman, Max 48, 49, 53, 55
Newton, Isaac 18, 23
nitrates 42–43

O

Oersted, Hans Christian 25, 36, 41
On the Economy of Machinery and Manufactures 22
On the Generation of Animals 6

P

Pascal, Blaise 19
Perkin, William Henry 43, 47
phonograph 31
photoautograph 34–35
photophone 38
Plato 4, 5, 9
Plato's Academy 5
polio 56–60
Pope, Sir William 46
Principia Mathematica 48
Prony, François de 20

R

Reed, Walter 61
Rivers, Thomas Milton 61
Robbins, Frederick 58, 61
Roebuck, John 13
Roosevelt, Franklin D. 58
Russell, Bertrand 48, 49, 55

S

Sabin, Albert 60, 61
Sabin vaccine 60
Salk, Jonas **56–61**
Salk vaccine
Savery, Thomas 12, 17
Scheutz, Edvard 20
Scheutz, Georg 20
Shockley, William 40
Smith, Adam 19
Socrates 5
Sprengel, Herman 30
Stephenson, George 17
steam engines 10–14
sugar lump vaccine 60
Swan, Joseph 30, 31, 33

T

telegraph 25–26
telephone 35–37
Thales of Miletus 4
Theophrastus 4, 9

Torricelli, Evangelista 10, 13
transistor 54
Trevithick, Richard 14, 15, 17
Turing, Alan **48–55**
Turing Test 53

U

Universal Stock Printer 27
Universal Turing Machine 50

V

Vitascope 30
Viviani, Vincenzo 13
Volta, Alessandro 33

W

Watson, Thomas Augustus 36, 41
Watt, James **10–17**
Weller, Thomas 58, 61
Western Union 38–39
Westinghouse Electric Company 32
Westinghouse, George 30, 32
Wheatstone, Charles 25
Whitehead, Alfred North 48, 49, 55
Wilkinson, John 17
World Wide Web 54
Wright, Orville 33, 41
Wright, Wilbur 33, 41